HOW TO MAKE ENCHANTING MINIATURE TEDDY BEARS

HOW TO MAKE
ENCHANTING
MINIATURE
Teddy Bears

DEBBIE KESLING

NORTH LIGHT BOOKS

Cincinnati, Ohio

How to Make Enchanting Miniature Teddy Bears. Copyright © 1997 by Deborah L. Kesling. Printed and bound in China. All rights reserved. No part of this book may be reproduced in any form or by any electronic or mechanical means including information storage and retrieval systems without permission in writing from the publisher, except by a reviewer, who may quote brief passages in a review. Published by North Light Books, an imprint of F&W Publications, Inc., 1507 Dana Avenue, Cincinnati, Ohio 45207. (800) 289-0963. First edition.

Other fine North Light Books are available from your local bookstore, art supply store or direct from the publisher.

01   00   99   98   97   5   4   3   2   1

Library of Congress Cataloging-in-Publication Data

Kesling, Debbie.
    How to make enchanting miniature teddy bears / Debbie Kesling.—1st ed.
        p.   cm.
    Includes index.
    ISBN 0-89134-738-0 (alk. paper)
    1. Soft toy making.   2. Teddy bears.   3. Miniature craft.   I. Title.
TT174.3.K47   1997
745.592′43—dc21   97-1599
                                                                                CIP

Edited by Julie Wesling Whaley
Production Edited by Michelle Kramer
Cover and interior designed by Brian Roeth
Cover photography by Pamela Monfort Braun/Bronze Photography
Photographs © John D. Kesling; line art/patterns © Deborah L. Kesling
The permissions on pages 116-117 constitute an extension of this copyright page.

North Light Books are available for sales promotions, premiums and fund-raising use. Special editions or book excerpts can also be created to specification. For details, contact the Special Sales Manager, F&W Publications, 1507 Dana Avenue, Cincinnati, Ohio 45207.

DEDICATION

For my mom, Janice Martin, with love . . .

ACKNOWLEDGMENTS

The global teddy bear community is such a warm and sharing place that properly recognizing all those I need to thank would fill an entire book! Fortunately, I am surrounded by loving, supportive friends and family, without whom I could never have completed this project.

BIG BEARHUGS . . .
To my husband John, for his incredible photography skills and for teaching me about "undelete." To my extraordinarily talented stepson Brady, for our midnight talks and "mind melds." To the contributing artists, who went to great lengths to send their wonderful creations to me from all corners of the globe. To my customers, for their collective patience. To Terri Effan, for coming to my rescue more times than I can count. To Dickie Harrison, for her encouragement. To my best friend, Sandy Humanski, for understanding when I didn't call, write or visit for months at a time. To my Internet Cybear-family, who provided support and encouragement throughout this project (especially Carolyn Whelpley, Janet O'Brien, Lee Kiat Seng and artist Jutta Cyr). To David Lewis and Argie Manolis, for believing in me. To the delightful Leyla Maniera, for her kindness and assistance. To my mom, Janice Martin, for being a living example of incredible strength and courage, and for believing in me as only a mother could. To my brother, bear artist Randy Martin, for being my "guinea pig." To my father, Roger Martin, for making a little girl believe that she could grow up to be anything she wanted. To Linda Mullins, for her invaluable help and encouragement. To A. Christian Revi, for playing the Wizard to my Cowardly Lion and helping me to find my courage. To Terrie Stong, for introducing me to Argie Manolis (and for a million other reasons!). To my darling Quimby, for knowing when I needed to laugh and making it possible. And to my editor, Julie Whaley, for her limitless patience, understanding and guidance.

ABOUT THE AUTHOR

 Debbie Kesling began making bears in 1983. Her work has been featured on the cover of *Teddy Bear Review* magazine and in many other books and periodicals. She has also been awarded a Golden Teddy for her miniature designs. Her instructional video, "Secrets of Miniature Bear Artistry," has sold thousands of copies worldwide since its 1994 release. Debbie has been honored to be an artist invited to participate in the Walt Disney World and Disneyland Teddy Bear Conventions. Some of her miniature designs have been produced by "Little Gems."

As a regular contributor to *Teddy Bear and Friends* magazine, Debbie writes the "Cybearspace" Internet column. She was also a contributing writer for *The Teddy Bear Sourcebook*.

Apart from writing and creating teddy bears, Debbie is passionate aviculturist and nature lover. Her parrot behavior modification techniques have been cited in many reference works, and her articles on endangered cockatoo breeding and behavior have appeared in several publications. Debbie makes her home in Lambertville, Michigan, with her husband John, her Irish Wolfhound Bubba and some feathered friends.

TABLE OF CONTENTS

Introduction   10

SECTION ONE

Bear Basics   11

A Brief History of the Teddy Bear

What Is a Miniature Bear?

The "Bear" Necessities

Tools

Bear Construction

Grooming

Repairing Damage—Reflocking

SECTION TWO

Bear Projects   33

Project One: Teddy Bear Pin

Project Two: Simple Teddy

Project Three: Posy Bear

Project Four: Roly-poly Bear

Project Five: Basic Jointed Bear

Intermission

Project Six: Jester Bear

—includes mini-project, Making a Poupard

Project Seven: Panda

Project Eight: Santa Bear

—includes mini-project, Making the Toy Sack and Tiny Bear

Project Nine: No-no Bear

Project Ten: Bunny

SECTION THREE

Bear Business—
Selling What You Make 89

Naming Your Business

Business Cards

Hang Tags

Pricing

Brochures

Getting the Word Out

Wholesale vs. Retail

SECTION FOUR

Bear Gallery 100

Thirty-one original bears made by artists around the globe. Take a look—they will inspire you! (Includes information on contacting the artists.)

Afterword 119

Appendix A: "Photographing Miniatures," by John Kesling 120

Appendix B: Sources for Supplies 121

Organizations for Teddy Bear Lovers 122

Suggested Reading 123

Index 124

*M*iniature teddy bears—tiny treasures with the power to enchant! What makes these wee bruins so appealing? Maybe it's because they can hide in a pocket, always ready to share a secret. Perhaps it's their ability to comfort at least as much as their full-size cousins. Could it simply be because they seem magical?

I've been making miniature bears for many years, and I still get a thrill when someone asks, "How do you *do* that?" The truth is, anyone can make tiny teddies. A little time, a lot of patience, some fuzzy fabric and a snippet of thread—combine these ingredients with the information in this book, and you too will be able to charm everyone with your "magical powers!"

I began my teddy bear career by making full-size teddy bears from mohair. They were very well received. I sold everything I could make and took orders for more! The only drawbacks were the cost of the mohair and the stress on my wrists from stuffing these big bears. Mohair is imported from England and Germany, and in the late 1980s prices jumped dramatically. I could get five or six 13″ (33cm) bears from one yard, but with prices running up to $120 per yard for the better fabrics, I was investing a lot of money in each bear I made.

At a teddy bear convention in Timonium, Maryland, I was fascinated with the few miniature bears I found. I was hooked instantly! On the ten-hour drive home, I started a to-do list. Item number one: Make a miniature bear. Little did I realize what a journey I was beginning!

I started by shrinking my full-size bear patterns with a reducing copier. I experimented with fabrics. I figured out how to make my own enameled eyes. I even produced a miniature "no-no" mechanism, which I share with you in project nine. When I decided I didn't like string-jointing, it took me eighteen months to develop an easy and reliable jointing method for bears 2″ (5cm) and less.

To inspire you, I feature the work of several international artists in section three of this book. Some names may be familiar to you, but the vast majority will not. These bears were selected to illustrate the wide variety of styles that exist in the teddy bear world. I don't want you to feel your bears must look like mine to be good: There are no bad bears, there is only bad workmanship! If you design with your heart and take care with your stitches, you will make wonderful bears!

Within these pages, I reveal to you every trick, tip and technique that I have gathered over the years. Nothing is reserved. No *secret methods* are withheld. I offer this to you because, for me, the only aspect of creation more joyful than the creation itself is teaching others to create for themselves.

Bear Basics

A Brief History of the Teddy Bear

Imagining a world without teddy bears is difficult, but these fuzzy friends have only existed since 1902. Two schools of thought exist regarding the birth of the teddy bear. I offer both in the spirit of fairness.

THE IDEAL TOY COMPANY

According to one version, it all began with a president. While Theodore Roosevelt and his entourage were in Mississippi to help settle a boundary dispute, they organized a recreational bear hunt. It seems the hunting party had little success in rounding up a bear for the president to "hunt down." A bear cub (or ailing bear, in some versions) was found and tied to a tree so that Roosevelt might shoot it for publicity photos. He refused.

Political cartoonist Clifford Berryman picked up on the incident and published a cartoon that depicted the president "Drawing the line in Mississippi." This referred both to the bear hunt incident and the boundary dispute.

Morris Michtom, a Brooklyn businessperson, saw the cartoon as an opportunity. His wife Rose stitched up some bears on her sewing machine and they sold as quickly as she could make them. Morris contacted Roosevelt, asking for permission to call the toys "Teddy's Bears." The president responded positively, and the Teddy Bear was born. Within five years, Morris and Rose were overseeing the production of one mil-

This Ideal bear is from about 1907. Standing 14" tall, he sports golden mohair and black button eyes. This is thought to be one of the earliest Ideal bears.
Courtesy
Linda Mullins.

"DRAWING THE LINE IN MISSISSIPPI"
This is the Clifford Berryman political cartoon that some say started it all!
Photo courtesy Library of Congress

lion bears a year under the name Ideal Novelty Company. They are still in business today as the Ideal Toy Company.

MARGARETE STEIFF GMBH

Simultaneously in Germany, Margarete Steiff was creating a similar bear based upon her nephew Richard's designs. Margarete was running a small toy-making business that started with elephant-shaped pincushions that women were requesting for use as children's toys. Richard had been observing bears and he asked Margarete to turn the patterns he designed into bears. Reluctantly, she created the bears, called "Friend Petz."

The bears were nearly a total failure at the 1902 Leipzig Toy Fair. A buyer for F.A.O. Schwartz, however, ordered three thousand of the bears, renaming them "Teddy" to make them more appealing to the American market.

The success of these early Steiff designs is legendary. They made millions of bears, and many have survived to this day. Of course, if you are lucky enough to find one, you can expect to pay at least one hundred dollars per inch for him.

ARTIST BEARS

Artist-designed teddy bears are a relatively recent phenomenon. Beverly Port began showing her bears at doll shows in the 1970s. This was the beginning of the designer bear market. Handcrafted bears have become an incredible industry over the past two decades. Thousands of artisans worldwide are making bears to meet the demands of collectors.

Here is a representation of early Steiff bears ranging in size from 14" to 16". White and cinnamon mohair appear to be two of the most desirable colors in early Steiff bears.
Courtesy Linda Mullins.

TEDDY GIRL

In 1994, this rare 1904 Steiff sold for £110,000 (about $171,380 in U.S. dollars at the time) against an £8,000 (about $12,000 in U.S. dollars) estimate. This surpassed the previous record auction price for a teddy bear, set in 1989 when a Steiff auctioned by Sotheby's fetched £55,000 (about $82,500 U.S.). Teddy Girl is shown here with her Henderson tartan.
Photo courtesy Christie's South Kensington, London

What is a Miniature Bear?

In the early days of the teddy bear, manufacturers created many innovative designs. Bears that tumbled, hot water bottles disguised as bears and even teddy bear liquor flasks were all the rage! Fashionable women carried teddy bears with them wherever they went. Capitalizing on this trend, manufacturers created small bears that were easy to transport in a purse or pocket. Some were simple, tiny teds, but others concealed perfume bottles, compacts, sewing kits and more. These bears were 3-4″ (7-10cm) tall, and the German Schuco Company created most of them.

To be considered a miniature these days, a bear should conform to dollhouse scale, which is 1″ (2½cm) to every 1′ (30cm). In other words, a 1″ (2½cm) bear would represent a 12″ (30cm) full-size bear in miniature. That would put the upper limit of miniature bears at 3″ (7½cm), which would represent a 36″ (91cm) full-size bear. Though no hard fast rule governs this, *Teddy Bear Review* magazine has set the upper size limit for their Golden Teddy Awards miniature category at 3″.

The first miniature bear artist was, appropriately, Kimberlee Port, the daughter of Beverly Port. Soon to follow was Elaine Fujita-Gamble, April Whitcomb-Gustafson and Sara Phillips. The delightful bears they created paved the way for the hundreds of miniature artists who followed their lead.

SCHUCO MINIATURES
These bears hold a delightful secret! With their heads in place, it is impossible to tell that they aren't ordinary miniature bears.
Photo courtesy Christie's South Kensington, London

SCHUCO MINIATURES
With their heads removed, you can see that the pink bear conceals a small flask, and the green bear contains a compact and lipstick tube!
Photo courtesy Christie's South Kensington, London

The "Bear" Necessities

Much of the fun in making miniature bears is tracking down and accumulating the supplies and tools required. As you make more bears, you may find equipment and techniques not discussed here that work better for you. There are no rules when it comes to miniature bear artistry, so explore new methods as they occur to you.

Because these bears are so small, they magnify every mistake and shortcoming. The supplies you choose can make or break your bear. By using high-quality materials, you are one step closer to creating an appealing, marketable teddy bear.

MINIATURE BEAR FABRICS

Though artists can create tiny teds from just about any fabric imaginable, the fabric of choice is upholstery velvet. The good news is you can make about two hundred 2½″ bears from a one-yard piece. The bad news is this fabric can be difficult to find.

The most desirable upholstery velvet has a long pile that gives the illusion of being mohair or synthetic plush. Some fabrics have a sparkling look; others have a sheen. My favorites are "matte," having no sheen or sparkle at all. When photographed with no size reference, a well-designed miniature should appear to be a full-size version of the item. I find that the matte finish fabrics help create this illusion.

The back of the fabric is as important as the front of it. Proper

A wide variety of supplies is used in making miniature teddy bears. Hunting for new supplies is fun, and will often serve as inspiration for new projects.

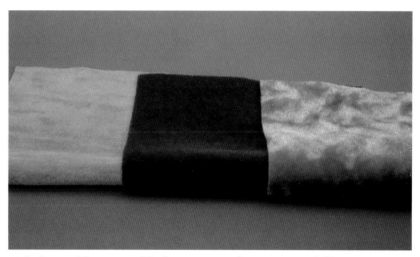

Upholstery fabrics suitable for miniature bears are available in a variety of finishes.
left to right: matte fabric, fabric with a slight sheen and sparkley fabric.

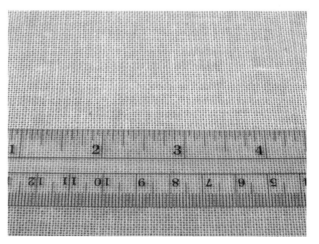

Upholstery fabric with crosshatch backing is preferred. You can use the squares as a guide for your stitching.

Synthetic suede is available in many different colors. It hides stitches nicely, and its flexibility makes it perfect for creating outfits and accessories.

Thread is used for sewing pieces together, stitching noses and mouths and as decorative trim. Keep a wide variety on hand.

backing has a crosshatch pattern of threads which makes the fabric easy to stitch. It is also flexible, which is very important when you are turning tiny arms and legs right-side out.

Finding appropriate fabrics is a challenge. By networking with other artists, you can usually find someone who has what you are looking for. When you do find some great fabric, buy much more than you think you need. Most artists don't want to sell the extra fabric they have, but they are very willing to trade it for something they don't have already.

These fabrics are very sturdy, so you can dye and wash them without harm. Some fabrics you find may be stiff due to the sizing applied during the manufacturing process. To soften the piece, run it through a wash cycle and use a liquid fabric softener.

Synthetic suede is ideal for pawpads, footpads and inset muzzles. If making very tiny bears, you can even use it for the entire project. It is available in an ever changing array of colors and is extremely easy to work with.

THREAD

New bearmakers often underestimate the importance of using the right kind of thread. Thread is an important piece of the puzzle. I have tried nearly every thread on the market and have found that most brands of extra fine thread work very well for stitching your bears together. Unfortunately, the color selection in most stores is quite limited. This means you must dye thread to match your fabric, or use regular weight sewing thread. I have used regular weight thread in many cases with satisfactory results, but, with the shorter napped fabrics, this makes it more difficult to conceal stitches.

Another option is transparent nylon thread. Depending upon the brand, you can get very pleasing results with it, though it does take some getting used to.

For trim and decoration, ultra-fine metallic and silk threads are perfect. You can transform single strands of embroidery floss into elaborate braiding. Use your imagination!

Always store your thread away from sunlight to prevent fading and weakening.

RIBBON AND TRIM

When searching for ribbon and trim for your little bears, think small. Pure silk ribbon is available in very narrow widths and gives an elegant touch to your creations. Dollhouse and miniature shows provide good hunting grounds for the search. Tiny beads can be used as buttons; lace edging becomes a pinafore; and chenille pipe cleaners are transformed into fur collars and cuffs. The possibilities are endless! For many bearmakers, the accumulation of trim and decoration for their bears becomes a near obsession.

JOINTING DISKS AND WIRES

I use plastic margarine container lids for joint disks, punching out the disks with a leather or hole punch. One lid will produce many disks. For the joint wires, I use jewelry headpins with a large head. These can be found at craft stores or through jewelry supply catalogs. The brass headpins are easier to work with and give a better joint than the silver-tone ones.

STUFFING

You can use regular polyester fiberfill or cotton batting for stuffing. I use cotton batting, as it stuffs the nooks and crannies of the tiny bear parts more solidly and doesn't "bounce back" like fiberfill. I have also used various types of shot (found in hunting and sporting goods stores) with the batting for a heftier feel. This simulates the pellet stuffing in full-size bears. I discourage the use of lead shot because of potential health risks. Tiny glass and plastic pellets are also available to achieve a "weighted" effect.

To give a bear a worn, loved look, I use excelsior (fine wood shavings sold in craft stores) in the feet and paws. By wearing away or cutting the foot and pawpads, the excelsior shows through, which is a delightful touch that simulates

Ribbons aren't just for tying bows. You can use them to make tiny outfits, too. As your miniature bearmaking progresses, you will find that you see everyday items with "new eyes."

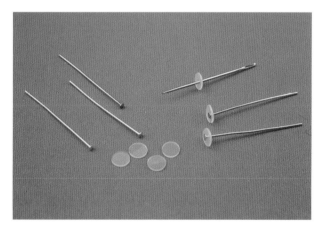

These disks were cut from margarine tub lids using a standard paper punch. The jewelry head-pins are inserted through the center of the disks to create a sturdy, simple joint.

A completed joint using plastic disks and headpins

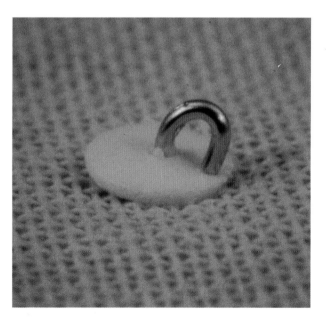

the look of antique bears. To keep it in scale, I chop it up first with an old pair of scissors.

EYES

Even with teddies, the eyes are the windows to the soul. A high-quality eye, properly placed, can give your bears that "take me home" look. I prefer using glass eyes, typically made in Germany. Each end of the eye wire is hand-dipped to create the glass balls of the eye. There is amazing size discrepancy, and you need to purchase many eyes to insure you can pair them up properly.

An excellent alternative is to use black onyx beads. They are uniform, and can give a good look. The smallest size I have ever found is 2mm, so using them for bears less than 2″ (5cm) tall is nearly impossible.

For the smaller bears, you can use black seed beads, but the result isn't very aesthetically pleasing. They are oblong, not round, and their size and shape vary even more than the glass eyes. You can make this less conspicuous by touching the fabric around the bear's eye area with a black, fine-tip permanent marker.

Another option is to make your own eyes. I did this for a couple of years, and it is fun, though tedious. Use jewelry headpins, enamel them with black automotive or model paint, and bake them very slowly at about 200°F (95°C). They look great, but if handled too roughly, the enamel will flake off.

Choosing the right size eye for your bear is a personal thing. I prefer an eye small in proportion to the head, and I suggest a rela-

Stuffing your bear is an integral part of the artistic process. Your choice of stuffing material will have a great impact on the final look and feel of your design.
stuffing materials (left to right): polyester fiberfill, plastic pellets, cotton batting

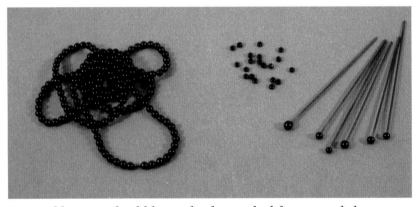

Your teddy's eyes should be as closely matched for size and shape as possible.
eyes (left to right): 2mm onyx beads, seed beads, glass eyes on wires

tive eye size for each project in this book. But you should select the size that gives you the look you want.

PLASTIC BAGS

Plastic storage bags are a necessity for most miniature artists. I use them for holding patterns, bears in progress, tiny bits of ribbon and lace—just about everything. A quart-size plastic storage bag will hold your bear parts, thread, scis-

sors and joints, making it very easy to take your bear work with you wherever you go.

PENS

Permanent marking pens are also necessary. When shopping for pens, take scraps of synthetic suede and upholstery velvet with you to test the pens. You'll need an ultra-fine point pen that dries instantly and doesn't bleed.

Another useful item is an

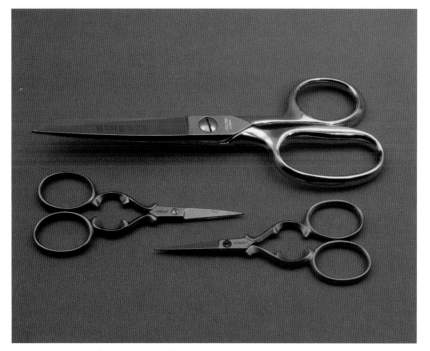

Scissors (top to bottom): Use large scissors for cutting big pieces of fabric, embroidery scissors for cutting out pieces and snipping thread and a second pair of embroidery scissors reserved exclusively for trimming faces.

opaque white marker or quilter's pencil. Seeing your tracings on fabrics dyed a dark color is difficult. By tracing with a white pen or pencil, you will save yourself a lot of frustration.

GLUE

It's a good idea to keep several types of craft glue on hand. Glue that is flexible and clear when it dries works nicely on the cut edge of ribbon to prevent fraying. You can also use it to reflock damaged areas on bears (see page 31).

Super adhesives can be just what you need for affixing trim to a bear, or for mounting a no-no mechanism. The standard types are too thin to control well, so I recommend the gel version.

Tools

The number of tools you will use in making your bears is amazing. These are some items I have accumulated in my personal bearmaking adventure. Note that the materials needed may change from project to project, but the basic tools stay the same. These tools are "given," and are not listed at the beginning of each project.

SCISSORS

One of the most important tools you will select is your scissors. You need full-size scissors for cutting large pieces of fabric, smaller ones for cutting the pattern pieces and a special pair of very tiny ones used only for trimming faces. Take good care of your scissors because you need a precise cut when working with little bears.

NEEDLES

For different areas of bearmaking, I use different size needles, all available at fabric craft stores and quilting supply stores. For sewing the pieces together, I like no. 12 quilting needles, although they can be too small for some people. Sharps are longer, but still have the slim profile you need. A needle that is too fat will cause your stitches and seams to show.

Beading needles are perfect for making ruffled collars and for some face-sculpting. Darning needles are handy for applying glue to the edges of ribbon or fabric to prevent fraying.

It's important to use high-quality needles, as the lesser needles on the market may have a rough eye. This will weaken your thread, causing it to pill and break.

HEMOSTATS, TWEEZERS AND SIDECUTTERS

I couldn't turn my sewn pieces without hemostats. I use the tiny-tipped, curved variety with great success, although you may like one of the other available styles. You can usually find hemostats in hobby stores, medical or veterinary supply catalogs and in some craft stores. Be certain to check how well the teeth fit together when in the locked position.

As with the hemostats, my tweezers are curved. Because I use mine for stuffing, I find the curved tip makes it easier to get the stuffing into the toes and paw tips. Tweezers are also handy for tying tiny bows and selecting beads from a container. I find mine at Amateur Radio hamfests, but I have also seen them at the same places that carry hemostats.

Not all people are comfortable stuffing with tweezers. They are sharp, and if you aren't careful you can poke them right through your fabric. Terri Effan, a meticulous miniature artist, uses an orange stick (available where cosmetics are sold). She sharpens one end to a point, and rounds the other end down. She uses this little tool for stuffing and turning. A couple of artists I know use toothpicks; still others use little screwdrivers.

Use sidecutters for cutting wires, such as excess eye or joint wire. I like my tiny pair, but I have been known to raid my husband's toolbox for a standard pair when I misplace mine. Also called *dykes*, sidecutters can be found at electronics supply stores.

BASKET TOOL

I use a modified basket tool for defining the ears on my 2″ (5cm) bears. For smaller bears, I use a scribe tool originally intended for use on ceramic or porcelain greenware (see page 30).

PUNCHES

For making joint disks, I use a hole punch. A standard paper punch makes disks suitable for a 2″ to 2½″ (5-7cm) bear. For bears smaller than this, I trim each disk by hand to the proper size. You can also use a leather punch for making disks. One type has a wheel that turns, allowing you to select the size disk you wish to make. I use a ⅛″ (31mm) punch to make the thread hole in my shrink plastic tags before baking (see page 55).

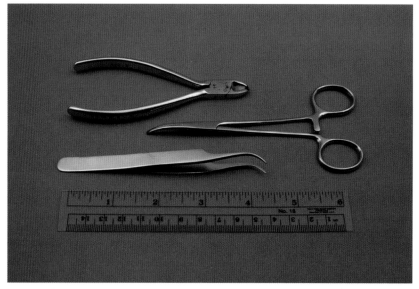

(top to bottom) Side cutters come in handy for cutting joint wires. Hemostats make turning tiny limbs right-side out much easier. Curved tweezers simplify the stuffing process. A rigid ruler will provide you with an accurate measurement of your bear's size.

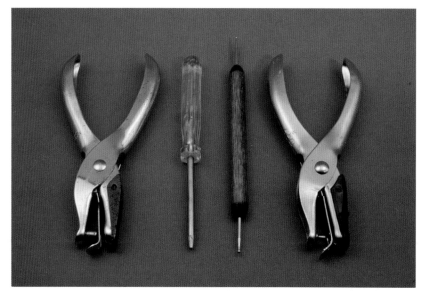

(left to right) A standard hole punch is used for punching joints from plastic. The modified basket tool and scribe tool, used in porcelain and ceramic work, help define the ears on various sizes of bears. A ⅛″ (approximately 3mm) hole punch is used to make a thread hole in shrink-plastic hang tags before baking.

Bear Construction

Here are some tips and techniques to help you in the creation of the projects in this book. From pattern preparation to stuffing, from eye placement to teddy bear repair, it's all here! These are the methods that work best for me.

PATTERNS

You can adapt most full-size bear patterns to miniature bear size. A quick pass through a reducing copier can usually handle the job. Because some copiers don't accurately maintain perspective, the resulting bear may be thinner and taller, or fatter and shorter, than the original.

I encourage you to use the patterns in this book to practice making miniature teddy bears. However, it is unethical and illegal to use these patterns to make bears for a profit. Unless a designer grants you permission to use her patterns, it is unethical to sell the bears made from those patterns. Before long you'll be designing your own bears to sell!

Make a copy of the pattern you want to use, then use rubber cement to affix the page to poster board. Cut the pieces out. The poster board gives you a good edge to trace around. Poke holes through the poster board using a darning needle at the joint markings, if applicable, so you can accurately mark the joint locations. These cardboard pattern pieces will wear with use, so you may wish to consider transferring the patterns to rigid plastic.

If you design a pattern you

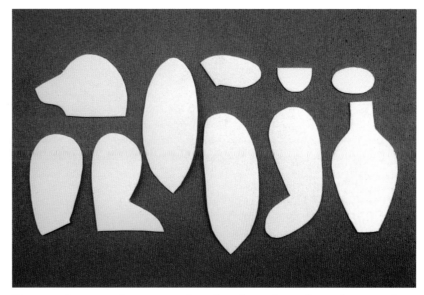

Pattern pieces cut from poster board such as those shown here work nicely—for a while. With use, the edges of the pattern collapse, causing inconsistencies in your design. If you plan to make several tracings of one pattern, it is best to transfer the pattern to something rigid, such as quilter's template material.

If you will be making numerous bears from one pattern, a set of rubber stamps is worth the investment. Make sure the pieces are lined up with all the arrows pointing in the same direction.

particularly like, or that you plan to recreate on a grand scale, you should consider having rubber stamps made. Not only does this eliminate the tedium of tracing, but the stamped image is more consistent than a traced image, resulting in a better bear. I recommend having two stamps made for a typical bear: one stamp for the fur pieces and a second one for the foot and pawpads. You can also make separate stamps for each body part, allowing you to mix and match your designs for added flexibility with less fabric waste.

When you order your rubber stamps, ask the vendor to supply you with a stamp pad large enough to accommodate your designs. The ink you use is also very important. I have had the best results using a product called Angels Ink, an industrial product. Your vendor can supply you with this as well.

LAYOUT, TRACING AND CUTTING

Because the fabrics used in bear-making have a nap, you must pay close attention to the layout of the pattern pieces. An arrow on the pattern shows the direction of the fabric nap. For most patterns, the general nap direction is down, although you can obtain charming results by varying this. The two pattern pieces that especially lend themselves to this variance are the head gusset and the ears.

On a miniature bear, every error is magnified. When tracing, follow the edge of the pattern pieces as closely as possible.

Most of the pieces require that you trace one, then flip the pattern piece and trace the second. Make certain you flip the piece horizontally and not vertically. After you flip a pattern piece, check the nap again to make sure it matches the direction of the nap on the first piece. This becomes second nature after you have completed a bear or two, but can be frustrating for the beginner.

When cutting the fabric, be careful not to cut the nap fibers. Be careful to work the blades of the scissors between the "hairs" right down at their base. This will help hide your seams. For the patterns in this book, cut right on the tracing lines. They require no seam allowance.

STITCHING

You will use three basic stitches for the projects in this book: the backstitch, ladder stitch and whipstitch. As you become more experienced, you may find other methods that work better for you. I use a single strand of knotted thread for most stitching. To illustrate these stitches, I have used a contrasting thread. When stitching your bears, use thread that is clear or matches your fabric.

I have written the instructions in this book for right-handed individuals. If you are left-handed, please make the appropriate adjustments.

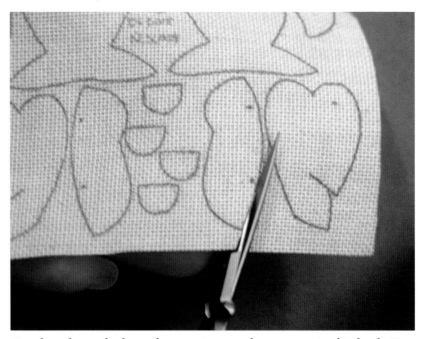

Cut directly on the line when cutting out the patterns in this book. Try to work your scissors between the fibers so you don't cut them. Snipped fibers along the cutting line will draw attention to your seams.

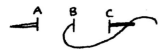

The Backstitch

Use this stitch for sewing the pattern pieces together. Remember, there are no seam allowances. Stitch as closely as you can to the edge of the fabric, using the squares on the backing of the fabric as your guide. This stitch will essentially weave the pieces together, giving a strong, uniform seam.

The method you use to begin and end each backstitch run is very important. When you turn the sewn body parts right-side out, the stitches at the opening are stressed. If you begin and end your stitches right at the opening, those stitches will have a tendency to come loose. To prevent this, you can begin your seam two squares over from where the opening will be (working right to left). Put two pieces of fabric together, fur sides facing in. Put your threaded needle through both pieces of fabric at point B. Reinsert your needle two squares to the right, at the point where your seam will start, C.

From this point on, it is simply "two squares over, one square back" (a backstitch) to the end of your stitching run. When you get to the end of the run, use the same technique to finish the seam as you did to start it: Use the "two squares over, one square back" method to stitch all the way to where you want the opening to be. Once there, backstitch into your already sewn seam and tie a knot. You never want your knot to be at the very beginning or end of a run.

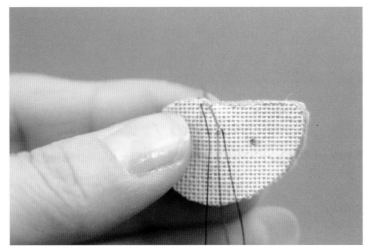

BACKSTITCH: STEP ONE

BACKSTITCH: STEP TWO

BACKSTITCH: STEP THREE

The Ladder Stitch

Use the ladder stitch for closing a bear after stuffing it, or for repairing ripped seams. This stitch, when properly executed, can give your bear a flawless finish. For this technique, always insert your needle from the back side of the fabric, coming out on the fur side.

Start at the bottom edge of a closing seam or tear that needs mending. Insert your needle through the back side of the fabric and come out the front. Move to the other side of the opening and, moving up about three backing squares, do the same thing. Return to the opposite side of the opening and repeat. Your stitches should never be directly opposite each other. The proper technique gives a sort of zigzag effect.

When you have completed three or four stitches, use your needle to press the raw edges of the fabric in toward the stuffing. Firmly—but carefully—pull your stitches tight. The seam will be nearly invisible. Continue this pattern to the end of the seam or tear.

At the end of your run, stitch a knot to the fabric. Insert the needle into the seam, coming out on the opposite side of the body part you are stitching. Pull firmly, then snip the thread close to the fabric (but avoid cutting any of the nap). This will bury your knot and give your closing seams a polished appearance.

LADDER STITCH: STEP ONE

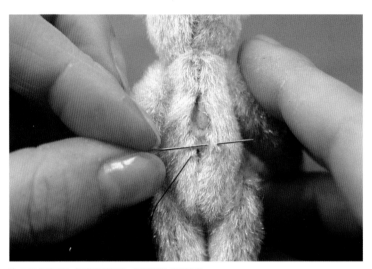

LADDER STITCH: STEP TWO

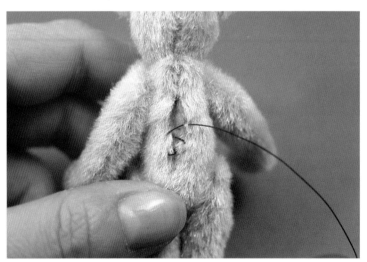

LADDER STITCH: STEP THREE
Take four stitches. Snug those up and take four more.

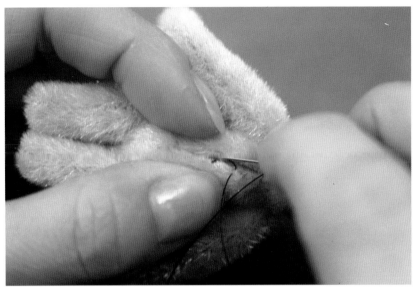

LADDER STITCH: STEP FOUR
Press the fabric edges in with your needle.

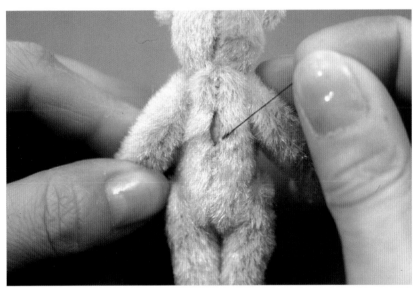

LADDER STITCH: STEP FIVE
Pull your stitches tight, and watch the opening vanish.

The Whipstitch

The whipstitch is primarily used for closing the raw edge of the ears and affixing them to the head. Insert your needle through the backing side of the fabric inside the ear at one end of the flat edge (the edge that sits against the head). This will hide the knot inside the ear. Hold the ear flat-edge-up and insert your needle through one side, coming out on the other (front to back). The remaining stitches will be just like the first, about three backing squares apart. When you get to the end of your run, tie a knot, but don't cut your thread. You will use the remaining thread to attach the ear to the head.

Running or Gathering Stitch

Use this stitch for gathering the neck around a head joint, or for gathering a collar, dress bodice or ruffle. The motion is somewhat like a dolphin (your needle) diving through the water (your fabric). Referring to the illustration, come up at A, and go down at B, up at C and down at D, and so on.

TURNING THE PIECES

One sentiment I hear repeatedly is that turning the sewn pieces right-side out is the most difficult aspect of miniature bearmaking. Using the proper tools and techniques can ease the stress of this step. In addition, knowing how to repair the inevitable mistake can

Turning the body is easier if you start at the bear's hump. Grab it firmly with your hemostats.

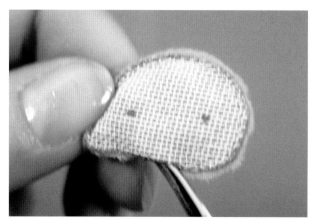

Peel the upper portion of the body right-side out by pulling slowly and carefully, adjusting your grip on the fabric if necessary.

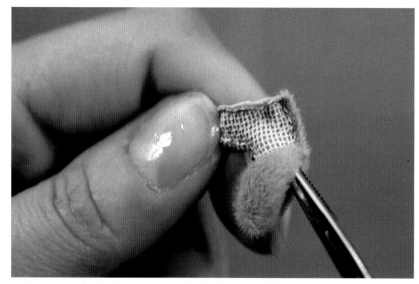

After turning the hip portion of the leg, carefully turn the foot right-side out.

help salvage pieces that might otherwise end in the trash. The basic procedure for turning each of a bear's parts is similar, but each piece has its own quirk that requires special treatment.

Turning the body piece is relatively easy. Insert your hemostats through the opening at the back of the body. Push it up toward the "hump" at the top of the back. Use your finger to push the hump into the open jaws of the hemostats. Lock the hemostats closed. Gently pull the top portion of the piece right-side out. Unlock your hemostats and insert them into the body piece again, this time grabbing the lower tummy area. Pull gently, and complete the turning process.

The main point of concern in turning the head is the tip of the nose. That is the best place to grab the piece for turning, but that is also the junction of several seams, making it a weak spot. Insert your hemostats into the neck opening of the head. Press the tip of the hemostats into the nose area. Use your finger to push the tip of the nose into the jaws of the hemostats, then lock the tool closed. Pull the head inside out very carefully! If you feel the tool slipping, stop and reattach it to the nose fabric.

The arms are very slender, which gives you little room to work the hemostats. Insert the tool into the arm opening and grab the tip of the paw. If the bear has pawpads, make certain you are grabbing both the furry top portion of the paw plus the pad. Pull gently until the forearm section is right-side out. Insert your tool again, this time grabbing the shoulder portion of the arm. Pull the top portion of the arm right-side out.

Although you have more room to work in the leg, the angles of the ankle and foot make this a tricky piece to turn. Insert your hemostats through the leg opening and grab the fabric at the hip. Carefully pull the hip right-side out.

Reinsert your tool and grab the toe area of the foot. If the bear has footpads, make sure you grab both fur fabric and footpad material. Lock your tool closed and very slowly pull the foot right-side out. If you meet with resistance part way, or if you feel your tool slipping, reattach your tool to a greater amount of material.

The ears are easy to turn. Just insert your hemostats into the ear, then gently pull right-side out.

STUFFING

Think of stuffing as "sculpting from the inside out." How you stuff your bear will greatly determine its personality. Stuffing the body, shoulders, hips and nose firmly is particularly important. Stuff the rest of the bear evenly so it isn't lopsided.

Use small bits of stuffing material and create a pleasing shape for every part you stuff. Be careful not to overstuff, as this will make it difficult to stitch the piece closed. Also, if you stuff the head too firmly, you cannot seat the eyes properly.

MOUNTING AND SEATING EYES

Eye placement is a very personal thing. Decide where the eyes should be, placing tiny dots with a fine point permanent marker. A general rule for eye placement is to put the eyes at the point where the nose meets the face, in line with the sides of the nose.

For mounting eyes in a head with a standard gusset, I suggest using four strands of thread. Insert your needle into the back of the neck area, coming out on one side of one of your eye placement dots. Don't pull the thread tight, as a tail must be left for tying the eye in place. Thread your needle through an eye bead. Reinsert your needle on the other side of your eye placement dot, coming out close to your original entry point at the neck area. Two tails of thread that are long enough to tie together should be hanging from the head. Do not tie or cut the thread at this point. Attach the other eye in the same manner.

Now that you have attached the eyes, it is time to seat them into the head. So many bears could be improved just by seating the eyes more deeply! Proper eye placement and seating helps create a bear that "looks back at you." Tie the set of tails for one eye with a half knot. Do the same with the other set of tails. Pull the half knots tighter, working with one eye then the other, until the eyes are deeply and evenly seated. Pressing the eyes into the head with something flat is helpful. I use the flat end of tweezers for this task.

When you are satisfied with the look you have achieved, tie each set of tails with another half knot to keep them in place. Run each of the four tails back into the head at your original entry point, coming out anywhere at the top of the head. Pull the thread firmly, then snip it off close to the fabric.

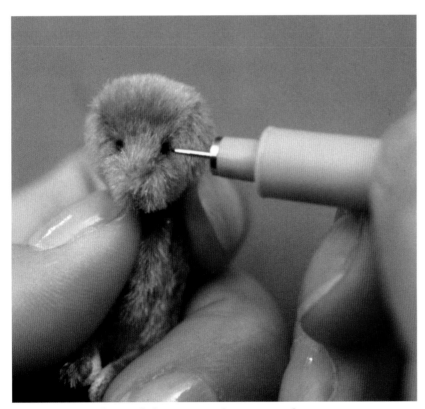

Use placement dots to help position the eyes evenly.

German style   *nostril*

horizontal   *vertical*

Insert your needle diagonally through the head from one side of the neck to the eye dot.

Seating the eyes deep in the head gives your bear a more pleasing and natural look.

Use something flat, like the flat end of tweezers shown here, to press the eyes into the head.

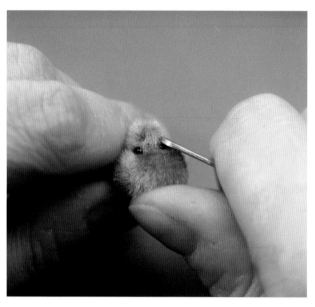

There is no right or wrong when it comes to noses. The only rule is that your stitches should be tidy and well executed. Here are some examples to get you started.

NOSE AND MOUTH

Stitching the nose and mouth can be a lot of fun! Do you want your bear to be happy? Sad? Silly? This is the step that injects life into your creation. I recommend you try for a symmetrical look, whatever style you settle on.

The type of thread you use for stitching your nose is very important. I like to use the ultra-fine threads for the nose and mouth, but these can be too fuzzy if you want a tailored look. Quilting thread that is 100 percent glaced cotton gives a smooth look, but may be too fat to use on bears smaller than 2½″ (6cm). One strand of embroidery floss will work, although it is also rather fuzzy.

You needn't use traditional colors for your bear's nose and mouth. You can match the nose color to the footpads, for example. You can outline a light colored nose with black thread to give it more definition. The perfect finishing touch for a clown is a multi-colored nose. For a very different look, try a nose stitched with metallic thread. Your only limitation is your own imagination!

EARS

Whipstitch the flat edge of the ear closed as described previously. Position the ear on the head in a pleasing spot and hold it in place with a needle. (Most pins are too fat, and can leave a visible hole in your bear's head!) Whipstitch the ear firmly to your bear's head. Do not tie a knot or cut the thread at the end of your stitch run. Instead, run the needle through the head, coming out at the other end of the ear.

Run your needle inside the ear between the two pieces of fabric, coming out on the seam about $\frac{1}{16}''$ (1-2mm) up the side of the ear. Insert your needle back into the head at the point on the head from which you just exited, coming out at the other end of the ear.

Run your needle inside the ear between the two pieces of fabric, again coming out on the seam, about $\frac{1}{16}''$ (1-2mm) up the side of the ear. Insert your needle back into the head at the point where you just exited, this time coming out at the center point of the ear. Pull the thread firmly, which will give the ear a natural, cupped look. Knot your thread, then bury it as you did with the eye threads. Use a scribing tool or dulled basket tool to help define the cup of the ear. Attach the second ear in the same manner.

Noses don't need to be black or brown. Be creative!

ATTACHING EARS: STEP ONE

Whipstitch the ear to the head, then run the needle back through the head to your starting point.

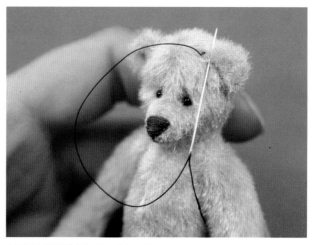

ATTACHING EARS: STEP TWO

Insert your needle between the ear pieces, coming out on the seam.

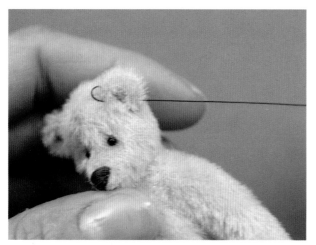

ATTACHING EARS: STEP THREE

Insert the needle at your starting point, coming out on the seam at the other end of the ear.

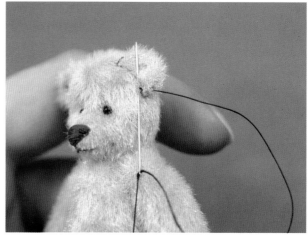

ATTACHING EARS: STEP FOUR

Insert the needle into the head at the edge of the ear. Come out at the center lower edge of the ear where it meets the head. Tie a knot, run the needle through the head and snip the thread at the exit point.

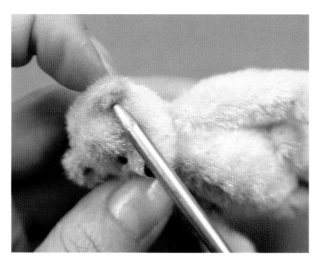

Use a scribe or other tool with a rounded tip to define the bear's ear. This gives a natural, cupped look that is quite appealing.

Grooming

A bear with nearly invisible seams has a special charm. If you have created a bear with solid seams, it will stand up to the grooming necessary to give a polished look. Using a wire brush or firm toothbrush, scrub the seams of your bear. Don't just brush him gently. You need to scrub hard. This will free all the fibers caught in the seams. The difference this one little step makes will amaze you!

Repairing Damage— Reflocking

No matter how many little body parts you have turned, mistakes are inevitable. If your hemostats slip, or if you pull a wee bit too hard, you can rip a seam or even pull the fur off the backing. Provided the damage isn't too extensive, you can do some things to repair it.

If you rip a seam, complete your bear as normal. After carefully stuffing the damaged body part, use the ladder stitch to repair the seam.

If you use eyes mounted on wires, it's easy to pull an eye right through the fabric, leaving a large hole. Use the ladder stitch to repair this damage, too.

You can reflock an area where you have pulled off the fur. Snip some fibers from matching fabric. Cut more fibers than you think you will need. Dip the point of a no. 12 needle into some craft glue and poke it repeatedly into the area on the bear where the fibers are missing. Reload the needle with glue as needed. Use tweezers to pick up the fibers you cut and stand them on end in the area you are repairing. Load the area with lots of fibers. After the glue has dried, blow on the area to remove the excess fibers. (See illustrations next page.)

IMPORTANT NOTE: The patterns in this book range from 1″ (2½cm) to about 3″ (5cm). If you don't feel comfortable starting out with bears this small, you can make the patterns bigger by using an enlarging copier. If you do enlarge the patterns, don't forget that you will also need to increase the size of the eyes you use.

Brush all of the bear's seams with a wire brush or stiff toothbrush for a nicely finished look. Scrub hard!

You can reflock an area where your bear has lost some fur.

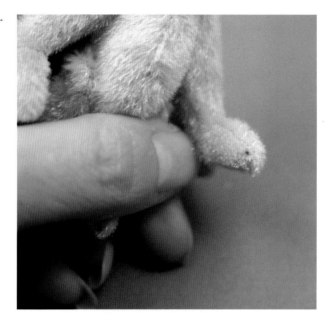

Apply craft glue to the affected area with a needle. Once the glue is applied, you must work quickly. Have your fibers cut and ready before applying the glue.

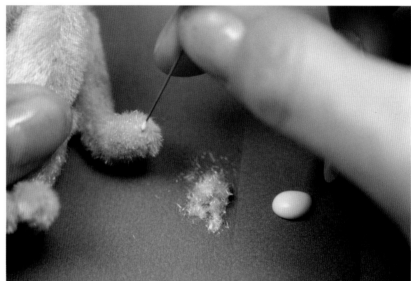

Apply the cut fibers using tweezers, standing them on end in the glued area. Allow the glue to set, then remove the excess fibers by blowing.

Bear Projects

Teddy Bear Pin

Our first project, the Teddy Bear Pin, is a simple start into the world of miniature teddy bearmaking. The pattern consists of only two pieces, and the project should take less than two hours to complete. Most teddy bear patterns include a gusset to give the head a fuller, more shapely appearance. To a certain degree, you may achieve a similar effect with the use of darts, as in this project.

MATERIALS

- small piece of upholstery fabric
- no. 12 quilting needle
- very fine, clear nylon thread *or*
- thread that matches your fabric
- black or brown thread for nose
- black, fine point permanent marker
- two 2mm (or smaller) black beads
- trim of your choice
- pinback
- backing plate (optional)
- cotton batting or polyester fiberfill

Layout and Cutting

Lay out the pattern pieces on your fabric, paying close attention to the direction of the fabric nap. Trace one side head piece, then flip the pattern over to trace the other side of the head. Trace four ear pieces (it takes two pieces to make one ear). Cut out the pieces, being careful to work your scissors underneath the fabric nap. Try to avoid cutting the nap fibers as much as possible. This will help hide your seams.

Sewing

Backstitch the dart (the V shape) on both head pieces using the squares of the fabric backing as a guide. By using the "two squares over, one square back" method discussed in section one (see page 23), your seams will be very sturdy and easy to conceal.

As shown in the pattern on the next page, place the head pieces fur sides together, then stitch from the back of the neck, A, around the top of the head and around the nose, finishing at the front of the neck, B. Remember to keep the neck area open for turning and stuffing. Tie a knot and cut your thread.

Place two of the ear pieces fur sides together and stitch around the rounded edge of the ear, leaving the flat edge open for turning. At the end of your stitching run, tie a knot, but do not cut the thread. Leave the tail of thread in place to use for attaching the ears to the head. Turn the ear right-side out and set aside. Stitch the remaining ear in the same manner.

Turning and Stuffing the Head

Turn the head right-side out, using your chosen tools. Stuff the head. Begin with the nose area, and stuff firmly. Remember to think of stuffing as sculpting from the inside out. While stuffing, view your bear head from all angles, working to make the head as symmetrical and well shaped as possible.

Close the neck area of the head

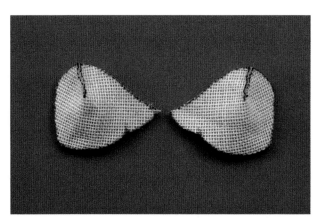

This is how the head pieces should look after the darts are stitched.

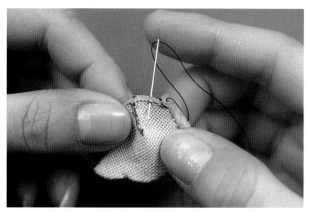

Stitch the pieces together, starting at the top back corner of the head.

using the ladder stitch, as explained in section one (see page 24). Once the closing is complete, run your needle back to the other end of the seam and take another stitch to pull in the corner of the neck. Do the same at the other end of the neck. Tie a knot and cut your thread.

Eyes

Mount and seat your bear's eyes as discussed in section one (see pages 27-28). Remember that there is no right or wrong to eye placement. It's a personal thing.

Nose and Mouth

Using techniques covered on pages 28-29, stitch the nose and mouth. I like to use very fine thread for noses and mouths, as it gives a more proportioned look than regular weight thread. Fine silk thread is easy to work with and has a lovely sheen.

Ears

Thread a needle onto the thread attached to one ear. Close the bottom (flat) edge of the ear using a whipstitch. Tie a knot at the end of your stitch run, but do not cut the thread. Attach the ears as described in section one (see pages 29-30).

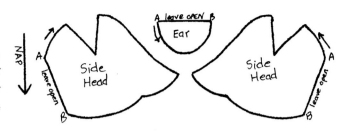

TEDDY BEAR PIN
Arrow indicates direction of nap
SIDE HEAD—*Cut one of each.*
EAR—*Cut four.*

Attaching Pinback and Trimming

Whipstitch your pinback to an appropriate spot on the bear head. The bear should be looking forward when he is pinned to your shirt, so orient the pinback accordingly. Of course, the pinback may be attached with craft glue or hot glue, but I find that glue isn't as reliable. Whatever method you choose, make sure the pinback is securely attached to the bear head.

For the pin pictured here, I added a jewelry backplate which I found at a craft store. If you decide to use a backplate, simply stitch your bear head to the front of the plate, then stitch the pinback to the back of the plate.

When trimming any of the bears in this book, the only limitations are your imagination and the items you can find. Let's nestle this bear head in a bed of tiny flower buds! Select some interesting artificial flowers of an appropriate size and snip the buds off, leaving as little stem as possible. Glue the buds around the perimeter of the bear head, framing the face. Use as few or as many as you like, but remember to allow room for pinning the bear to your shirt.

Cut lots of small leaves from the stems and glue them among the flower buds. If none of the leaves are small enough, cut your own small leaves out of the larger ones. You might even add some tiny bows, created with 2mm silk ribbon. What about adding some tiny pearl beads? For a feminine look, touch a cotton swab to powder blush. Scrub it very firmly onto the cheeks of your bear.

Simple Teddy

This little bear has no head gusset or pawpads, which makes assembly quick and easy. String jointing techniques make your bear's head and limbs moveable! I have used scraps of ribbon and two tiny buttons to create a simple pinafore for her, but you may dress your teddy any way you wish. Maybe your teddy will turn out to be a boy, or perhaps you would like a "bare bear."

MATERIALS

- small piece of upholstery fabric
- no. 12 quilting needle
- very fine, clear nylon thread *or*
- thread that matches your fabric
- black or brown thread for nose
- black, fine point permanent marker
- two 2mm (or smaller) black beads
- cotton batting or polyester fiberfill

SIMPLE TEDDY
Arrow indicates direction of nap
SIDE HEAD—*Cut one, reverse, cut second.*
EAR—*Cut four.*
BODY—*Cut one, reverse, cut second.*
ARM—*Cut two, reverse, cut other two.*
LEG—*Cut two, reverse, cut other two.*

Layout and Cutting

Lay the pattern pieces out on your fabric, paying close attention to the direction of the fabric nap. Trace carefully, and do not forget to flip the pattern pieces where indicated! Cut the pieces out exactly on the tracing line. No seam allowance is needed.

Sewing

All pieces are sewn fur sides together, then turned right-side out. Start by backstitching the two body pieces together from A to B in the direction of the arrow. Stitch as closely as possible to the cut edge of the fabric. Leave the back of the body open for turning

and stuffing as shown on the pattern.

Backstitch along the darts (the V shapes) on each side head piece. Tie a knot and snip the thread. Place the head pieces fur sides together, matching up the darts. Stitch from the back of the neck, A, around the top of the head and around the nose, finishing at the front of the neck, B. Remember to keep the neck area open for turning and stuffing. Tie a knot and cut your thread.

Stitch the legs from point A to point B in the direction of the arrow. Leave the back of the leg open for turning and stuffing.

Stitch the arms together from A to B in the direction of the arrows. Leave the back of the arms open for turning and stuffing.

Place two of the ear pieces fur sides together and stitch around the rounded edge of the ear from A to B, leaving the flat edge open for turning. At the end of your stitching run, tie a knot, but do not cut the thread. Leave the tail of thread in place to use for attaching the ears to the head. Turn right-side out and set aside. Stitch the other ear together in the same manner.

Stuffing

Turn the body, arms and legs right-side out using the tools of your choosing. Stuff these parts firmly with polyester fiberfill or cotton batting. Close the openings on all these pieces using a ladder stitch as described on pages 24-25.

The Head

Turn the head right-side out, using tools with which you feel comfortable. Stuff the head firmly. You don't want the head to be so hard that you cannot pull the eyes down into it, but it must be stuffed firmly enough that it has a pleasing shape. Again, think of stuffing as an inside-out sculpting technique. The shape of your bear's head will greatly determine his ultimate personality.

Eyes

Using a very fine point marker, put a tiny dot at the spot where you want to mount each eye. Thread your needle with black thread, doubled or even quadrupled. You will need about a foot of doubled or quadrupled thread to work with for each eye. The thread you use must be able to handle much pulling.

Inserting the needle up into the neck opening, come out of the face at the point where you have placed one of the dots. Run the needle through the eye bead, then back into the face a fraction of an inch from where you came out. Come out anywhere in the neck opening. Tie both ends of the thread together in a half-knot, but do not cut the threads at this time. Do the same with the other eye.

To give your bear a pleasing look, you should try to seat the eyes deeply into the head. You can accomplish this by pushing on each eye with something flat, pressing it deeply into the face, then tightening the appropriate half-knot. Once both eyes are evenly seated, tie the thread tails from both eyes together in a tight double-knot. Clip the threads about 1″ (2.5cm) from the knot and tuck the tails into the head.

Jointing the Head to the Body

Using a needle and doubled thread, gather the neck opening with a running stitch. Pull the neck tightly closed, and tie a double knot. Do not cut the thread or remove the needle at this time. You will use this thread to joint the body to the head. Insert your needle in the top of the body at the point where you would like the head attached. Push the needle through the body, exiting at the back seam of the body. Reinsert the needle into the body, coming out at the neck again. Catch a bit of the bottom of the head with the needle. Repeat the process, pulling snugly as you go. Do this until the head feels securely attached, yet will pivot.

When you have achieved this, bring your needle out somewhere along the back seam on the body. Tie a knot, then run the needle through the body and out the front. Pull the thread snugly, then snip it close to the fabric. This will hide your knot.

Jointing the Legs and Arms

Decide where you want the legs to be. At the proposed "pivot point" on the body, insert your needle, running it through the body and out the other side at the corresponding point. Run your needle through a leg, back through the same leg, back into the body, out the other side, through the other leg and so on until the legs are firmly attached, yet still movable. Be sure the legs are facing front. (A teddy with his legs on backwards looks quite silly!) To finish, come out at the back seam on the body and tie-off, just as you did with the head. Joint the arms to the body in the same manner.

Nose and Mouth

Stitch your nose and mouth using the techniques on page 28.

Ears

You should have two ears with tails of thread attached. Thread a needle onto one tail and close the bottom (flat) edge of the ear using a whipstitch as described in section one. Tie a knot at the end of your stitch run, but do not cut the thread. Position the ear on the head in a pleasing spot, then hold it in place with a needle. Most pins are too fat and can leave a visible hole in your bear's head. Whipstitch the ear firmly to your bear's head. Do not tie a knot or cut the thread at the end of your stitch run. Instead, run the needle through the head, coming out at the other end of the ear.

Run your needle inside the ear between the two pieces of fabric, coming out at the seam about ¹⁄₁₆″ (1-2mm) up the side of the ear. Insert your needle back into the head at the point on the head where you just exited, coming out at the other end of the ear. Run

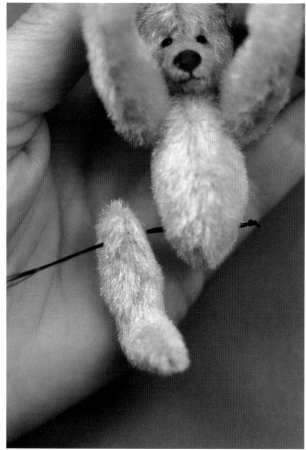

STRING JOINTING: STEP ONE
Run your needle through the body and one of the legs.

STRING JOINTING: STEP TWO
Insert your needle back through the leg and body, then through the second leg.

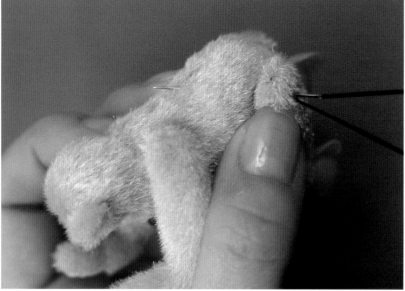

STRING JOINTING: STEP THREE
When both legs are secure, put your needle through a leg, coming out at the closing seam on the body. Tie a knot, then bury your thread.

your needle inside the ear between the two pieces of fabric, again coming out on the seam, about ¹⁄₁₆″ (1-2mm) up the side of the ear. Insert your needle back into the head at the point on the head where you just exited, this time coming out at the center point of the ear. Pull the thread firmly, which will give the ear a natural, cupped look. (See photos on page 30.) Knot your thread, then bury it as you did with the eye threads. Attach the second ear in the same manner.

Final Touches

Trim the face and muzzle area of your little bear with the embroidery scissors that you have set aside just for face trimming. Trim carefully around the eye area, snipping any long or stray fibers that interfere with the twinkle in your bear's eyes. Trim around the mouth threads so your teddy's smile will show. To give the illusion of pawpads, trim the fur from the pad area on the arms. Brush all the seams with a small wire brush or a toothbrush.

Adorn your little fellow with a simple bow around his neck, or create a spectacular collar. The way your teddy is decorated is a wonderful way to put your personal stamp on your creation.

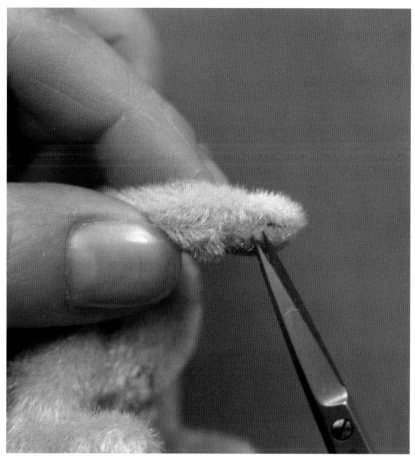

Trimming the fibers from the paw area on the inside of the arm gives the illusion of inset pawpads.

Posy Bear

Posy Bear is a fun project that introduces the head gusset. Posy's head is surrounded by silk flower petals and mounted on florist's wire, then "planted" in a tiny terra cotta flower pot.

MATERIALS

- small piece of upholstery fabric
- no. 12 quilting needle
- darning needle
- very fine, clear nylon thread *or*
- thread that matches your fabric
- black, brown or orange thread for nose
- black, fine point permanent marker
- yellow liquid dye (optional)
- two 2mm (or smaller) black beads
- cotton batting or polyester fiberfill
- thin, green florist's wire
- margarine tub lid
- standard hole punch
- craft glue
- small, terra cotta flower pot (about ¾" or 2cm diameter) from a doll-house shop
- silk flowers of any type, about 1" across
- imitation grass or mulch from a dollhouse shop
- silicone caulk or hot glue
- powdered blush (optional)
- cotton swabs (optional)
- pinback (optional)

Dyeing Fabric

I like using a bright, sunny yellow fabric for Posy, but it is not easy to find yellow upholstery fabric. To get a color you really like, you can dye light colored fabric to suit your needs. I recommend washing any fabric before you use it, but washing is particularly important before dyeing. Run your fabric through a normal wash cycle, using the detergent of your choice. You can use fabric softener if you wish. Toss the fabric into the dryer on the permanent press setting.

After washing, cut some squares for dyeing. The squares should be a manageable size, about 5″ × 5″ (13cm × 13cm). Soak the fabric in warm water until it is thoroughly wet to help it absorb the dye. Heat some water in a saucepan on the stove, then add your dye. Keep the burner on low during the entire dyeing process. I like using liquid dyes because you don't have to worry about any undissolved color granules. Always err on the light side: It is much easier to add dye for more intense color than to try to remove excess color. You can add a dash of table salt to your dye bath to help fix the color.

Place your fabric square in the dye bath, keeping it in constant motion with tongs. Keep a very close eye on the color of your fabric by lifting it out of the dye batch periodically. Remember, some fabrics accept dye almost instantaneously, while others need quite a while to achieve the desired hue.

When you are pleased with the color, remove the fabric square from the dye bath and hold it under cold running water. This removes the excess dye and helps to set the color. Squeeze the water from the fabric, then hold it under the cold water again. Repeat this process until the water you squeeze from the fabric is clear. Dry the fabric in the dryer.

It is a good idea to take notes while you are dyeing fabric to help you recreate the color in the future. Write down how much water you used, how much dye you added and how long the fabric was in the dye bath.

Layout and Cutting

Lay the pattern pieces out on your fabric, paying close attention to the direction of the fabric nap. Trace carefully, and cut the pieces out exactly on the tracing line. No seam allowance is needed.

The head gusset gives you more control over the shape of the head. By altering the width of different parts of the gusset you can fine-tune your designs. The nap direction for the gusset is arbitrary, although I tend to prefer the nap running down toward the nose. For very traditional designs, you may want the nap to run upwards instead.

Sewing

As with all other projects in this book, the pieces are sewn fur sides together, then turned right-side out. Start by sewing the two side head pieces together from A to B in the direction of the arrow. Stitch as closely as possible to the cut edge of the fabric. When you reach point B (the nose area), tie

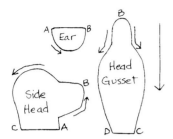

POSY BEAR
Arrow indicates direction of nap
SIDE HEAD—*Cut two. (Trace one, reverse, trace second.)*
EAR—*Cut four.*
HEAD GUSSET—*Cut one.*

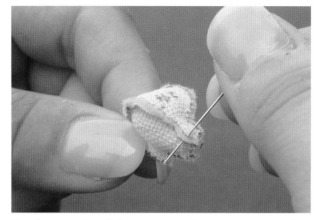

Stitch one side of the gusset to the appropriate side head piece from the nose to the back of the neck. Stitch the other side of the gusset to the remaining side head piece in the same manner.

a knot, but do not cut your thread.

Position your head gusset as shown. Stitch the gusset to the side head piece from your knot, B, to the back of the neck, C. Tie a knot and cut your thread. Re-knot your thread and stitch the other side of the head gusset to the remaining side head piece from B to the back of the neck, D (on the gusset). Tie a knot and cut your thread. Because of the head gusset, there is no need for darts.

Place two of the ear pieces fur sides together and stitch around the rounded edge of the ear from A to B, leaving the flat edge open for turning. At the end of your stitching run, tie a knot, but do not cut the thread. Leave the tail of thread in place to use for attaching the ears to the head. Turn right-side out and set aside. Stitch the other ear together in the same manner.

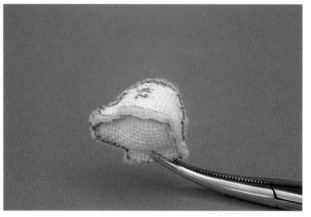

Here is the completed head with gusset in place before turning right-side out.

Stuffing and Eye Placement

Turn the head right-side out, using tools with which you feel com-

Drawing eye placement dots with ink makes it easier to mount eyes evenly.

fortable. Stuff the head firmly. The addition of a head gusset creates more nooks and crannies you will need to stuff. Pay particular attention to the nose, cheeks and temple area. View the head from all angles while stuffing to make it as symmetrical as possible. Brush all the seams thoroughly. Mount and seat the eyes as described on pages 27-28 and in the previous projects. A good spot to place the eyes is on the gusset seams, at the point where the gusset widens.

Mounting the Head

Use the standard hole punch to cut a disk from the margarine tub lid. Poke a hole in the center of the disk with the darning needle. Push one end of the florist's wire through the hole in the disk. Make a loop at the end of the wire to hold the disk in place. Insert the disk into the head through the neck opening.

Using a needle and doubled thread, gather the neck opening with a running stitch. Pull the neck tightly closed and tie a double knot. Make sure the florist's wire is centered in the neck opening. Tie a double knot and cut your thread.

Run the florist's wire through the hole in the plastic disk.

Use your hemostats to bend a loop at the end of the wire. This will hold the wire in place inside the head. I have trimmed some of the threads from the wire so you may see the loop more easily.

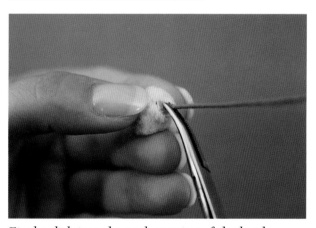

Fit the disk into the neck opening of the head.

Use a running stitch to gather the neck fabric around the wire.

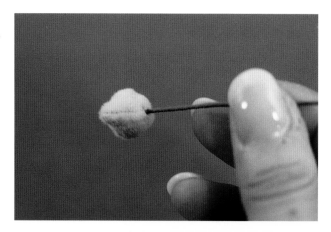

Outlining a light colored nose with contrasting thread provides definition.

Nose and Mouth

Stitch your nose and mouth using the techniques covered in section one of this book. To make the features more distinct and fanciful, I recommend using orange or gold thread for the nose. A nice touch is to outline the colored nose with thread of a contrasting color. Use black or brown thread for the mouth.

This is a good time to trim Posy's face. Trim any stray fibers carefully, using techniques described in previous projects. Pay close attention to the areas around her eyes, nose and mouth.

Shading

A touch of powdered blush gives extra dimension to your Posy, and adds to the whimsical flavor of the design. Using a cotton swab, scrub a small amount of blush on the cheek area of the face. Scrub firmly to work the blush all the way into the fabric backing.

Ears

Attach the ears as described in the previous projects. If you have decided to add blush to Posy's cheeks, you can also add a bit to the inside of her ears. This gives her a nice, balanced look and again adds to the whimsy.

Slip the silk flower petals onto the neck wire.

Taking the time to arrange the petals around the bear's face is well worth the effort.

"Planting" Posy

You can make Posy any type of flower you wish. It may be easier for you to purchase your flowers after you have reached this point in your project. By taking your completed "head-on-a-wire" to a craft store, you will better be able to judge which size, shape and color petals will look best.

Once you have selected your flower, disassemble it to the point that you have a collar of petals to nicely frame your bear head. The petals will typically have a center hole, through which you can thread the wire that protrudes

Fill the flower pot with clear silicone caulk or hot glue. You want it to look like a real flower pot, so make sure you leave some space at the top for your mulch.

from the head. Once the wire is threaded through the petals, use craft glue to affix the petals to the bottom of the head. Discreetly placed bits of glue will also help in arranging the petals around the face of your bear head.

When you are satisfied with the look you have achieved, snip the florist's wire to an appropriate length. Fill the pot with silicone caulk or hot glue. Don't fill the pot to the rim, as you need space for your "mulch."

Stand the stem in the center of the terra cotta pot. Once the caulk or glue has set, you won't be able to move the wire. Press imitation grass or mulch onto the surface of the caulk or glue while it is still quite sticky. This will be Posy's "soil."

You may add a pinback to the terra cotta pot if you wish to wear this project as a pin. Posy is also a cute accessory for a larger bear to hold! Imagine a 4″ (10cm) gardener bear with apron, gardening tools and seed packets holding this little bruin-in-bloom! You could create an entire garden of Posies using different flowers.

Full-Bodied Posy

One design option for this project is to create full-bodied Posy. Using the pattern from project five, make Posy a body, arms and legs from green upholstery fabric. She can be displayed in a small, terra cotta pot, too!

Insert the stem of your Posy Bear into the center of the pot.

While the caulk or glue is still sticky, add your imitation mulch. Press it firmly into place, making certain there are no bare areas.

You can create a full-bodied Posy by making a body with green upholstery fabric. Use a larger flower pot for the bear to stand in.

Roly-poly Bear

You may remember having a roly-poly toy when you were a child. I was always fascinated with tipping mine over, only to have it spring right back up. Roly-poly bears have been made by various manufacturers since the early 1900s. This project is, of course, in miniature. Properly stuffed, it will function just like its larger cousins. This bear is string jointed.

MATERIALS

- small piece of upholstery fabric
- no. 12 quilting needle
- darning needle
- very fine, clear nylon thread *or*
- thread that matches your fabric
- trim of your choice
- black, fine point permanent marker
- black or brown thread for nose
- two 2mm (or smaller) black beads
- craft glue
- small shot, or 1mm pellets
- cotton batting or fiberfill

Pattern and Layout

The roly-poly pattern doesn't look much like a bear, does it? His body has several short darts to give it a pear-like shape. The round circle goes into the bottom of the body as a base. His arms are somewhat short, giving him a "baby bear" look, and he has no legs.

Sewing

As with all other projects in this book, the pieces are sewn fur sides together, then turned right-side out. Start by sewing the two side head pieces together from A to B in the direction of the arrow. Stitch as closely as possible to the cut edge of the fabric. When you reach point B (the nose area) tie a knot but do not cut your thread.

Stitch the gusset to the side head piece from your knot, B, to the back of the neck, C. Tie a knot and cut your thread. Knot your thread again and stitch the other side of the head gusset to the remaining side head piece from B to D. Tie a knot and cut your thread. Because of the head gusset, there is no need for darts.

Fold the arm piece in half, then stitch the arms from A to B. Tie a knot and cut your thread. Complete the arm seam by stitching from C to D. The area between B and C is left open for turning and stuffing.

Place two of the ear pieces fur sides together and stitch around the rounded edge of the ear from A to B, leaving the flat edge open for turning. At the end of your stitching run, tie a knot, but do not cut the thread. Leave the tail of thread in place to use for attaching the ears to the head. Turn right-side out and set aside. Stitch the other ear together in the same manner.

There are three sections to the body, though it is all one piece. The middle section will be the front of your bear. Stitch the two large darts and five smaller darts (V shapes in the pattern) on the body.

Fold the body in half and stitch it together from the neck, A, to the upper back, B. Tie a knot and cut your thread. Stitch from point C to point D. The gap between points B and C is for turning and stuffing.

Insert the round base piece into the bottom of the body and stitch into place. I prefer positioning it so that the nap runs towards the back of the bear.

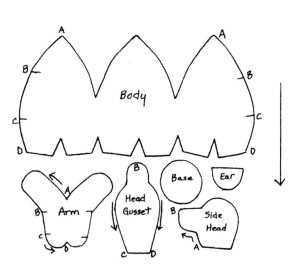

ROLY-POLY BEAR
Arrow indicates direction of nap
BODY—*Cut one.*
ARM—*Cut two.*
HEAD GUSSET—*Cut one.*
SIDE HEAD—*Cut one, reverse, cut second.*
BASE—*Cut one.*
EAR—*Cut four.*

Stuffing the Head and Arms

Turn the head right-side out, using tools with which you feel comfortable. Stuff the head firmly, as discussed in project three (see pages 44-45). View the head from all angles while stuffing to make it as symmetrical as possible. Mount and seat the eyes as described in the previous projects. Stitch the nose and mouth. Gather and close the neck area of the head as covered in project two (see page 39). Sew the ears and attach to the head.

Turn the arms right-side out. Stuff with cotton batting and stitch closed.

Stuffing the Body

The roly-poly action of this fellow is totally dependent upon proper stuffing techniques. Lead shot works very nicely for these bears, but due to the danger in handling lead, I strongly discourage its use. Copper and steel shot can be found in various sizes, and it is much safer to work with. You may also use glass or plastic pellets. Glass pellets are three times as heavy as plastic and work better to achieve the roly-poly action in this project.

Turn the body right-side out. Place approximately ⅛ teaspoon of craft glue inside the body in the center of the circular base. Pour some shot or pellets into the body. Press it into the glue, forming the bottom of the body into a rounded, roly-poly shape. It should be slightly flattened at the

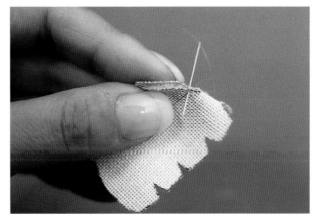

Stitch the roly-poly's body darts. The darts provide the necessary rounded shaping to make the roly-poly action possible.

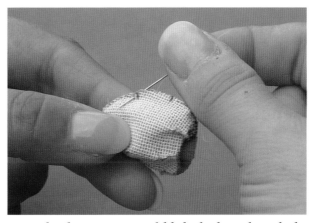

Once the darts are sewn, fold the body and stitch the back seam. Remember to leave an opening for turning and stuffing.

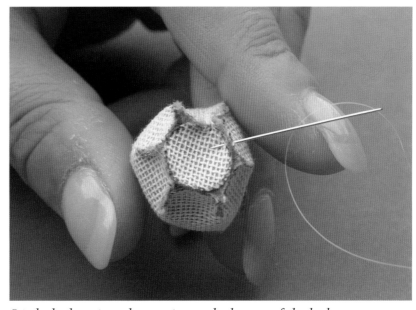

Stitch the base into the opening at the bottom of the body.

bottom, but rounded enough to easily tip over. Make sure the pellets or shot are evenly distributed, or your bear will not sit straight! Set the body aside and let the glue dry.

After the glue has set, stuff the rest of the body with cotton batting, checking the balance of the bear as you go. Set him on a table and tip him over. He should bounce back to an upright position. If he seems off balance, add a little extra batting or shot in the appropriate place.

Assembly

Brush all the seams thoroughly. Attach the head and arms to the body by string jointing as described in project two (see page 39). Stitch the back of the body closed. Through the entire assembly process, you need to keep checking both the physical and visual balance of your bear. His head and arms should be placed where they look best and don't interfere with the roly-poly action.

Trim

With a little imagination, roly-poly bears can be made to look like all sorts of characters (see "Pumpkin" on page 107). For this project, I have added simple adornment, but you can be as creative as you like!

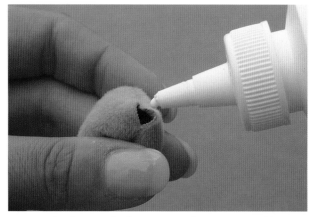

Use craft glue in the base to anchor your stuffing in place. It also gives the project a more rigid, solid bottom.

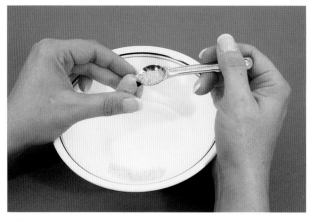

While the glue is still wet, fill the base area of the roly-poly with a weighty stuffing material, such as these recycled glass beads.

Look closely, and you can see the base insert in the bottom of this roly-poly. Note the symmetry of the body that is achieved through careful stuffing. The base insert is difficult to see because the seams have been vigorously brushed.

Basic Jointed Bear

With teddy bears, as with so many other things, the little extra touches make all the difference. This project introduces two techniques that will take your bearmaking to the next level: traditional joints and inset pads. Part of the charm of well-executed miniatures is that they mirror their full-size counterparts to an amazing degree. By using traditional joints and inset pads in your designs, your bears will have a "big bear" look that collectors find most desirable.

MATERIALS

- small piece of upholstery fabric
- small piece of synthetic suede for pads
- no. 12 quilting needle
- very fine, clear nylon thread *or*
- thread that matches your fabric
- black or brown thread for nose
- black, fine point permanent marker
- two 2mm (or smaller) black beads
- ten ¼" or 6mm plastic disks for joints
- five headpins for joints
- cotton batting or polyester fiberfill
- darning needle

Pattern and Layout

You will notice an important addition to this pattern: foot and paw-pads. Synthetic suede is commonly used as pad material in both large and small bears. It is very easy to work with and comes in an incredible array of colors. Trace the pattern (except the paw and footpads) onto upholstery fabric. Trace the paw and foot-pads onto synthetic suede.

BASIC JOINTED BEAR
Arrow indicates direction of nap
BODY—*Cut two. (Trace one, reverse, trace second.)*
LEG—*Cut four. (Trace two, reverse, trace two more.)*
SIDE HEAD—*Cut two. (Trace one, reverse, trace second.)*
INSIDE ARM—*Cut two. (Trace one, reverse, trace second.)*
OUTSIDE ARM—*Cut two. (Trace one, reverse, trace second.)*
PAWPAD—*Cut two.*
EAR—*Cut four.*
HEAD GUSSET—*Cut one.*
FOOT PAD—*Cut two.*

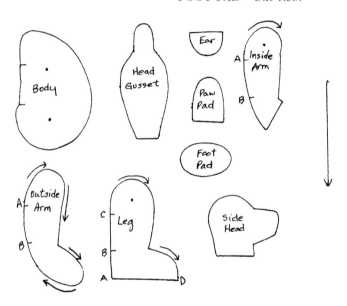

Sewing

Stitch the bear's head, body and ears as you did in the previous projects. You should stuff the head at this point, but do not stitch the neck area closed. The eyes, nose, mouth and ears will be added after jointing.

Don't fret about inserting the pads! It is easy once you see how the pieces fit together. For the pawpads, you are essentially replacing the palm of the bear's paw with synthetic suede. Because of that, you now have two fur pieces of different lengths for each arm. The shorter arm piece is the inner arm. The longer piece is the outer arm. Stitch a synthetic suede pad to each inner arm piece as shown.

Remembering that the pieces must be sewn right-sides-together, match up each inner arm with the appropriate outer arm. Sew each inner arm piece to its corresponding outer arm piece from A to B in the direction of the arrows.

Sew the legs in three stages. First, sew from the bottom of the heel, A, to point B. Next, sew from

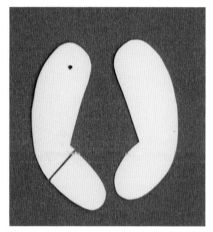

With the addition of pawpads, the arm now consists of three pieces: (clockwise, from right) outside arm, pawpad and inside arm. The pawpad is stitched to the inside arm, which is then sewn to the outside arm.

This is what the pawpad side of your completed arm will look like before and after turning.

Insert a footpad into the bottom opening of the leg. You may find it helpful to use a single stitch to anchor the pad in place at the toe and heel. Stitch the footpad in place, then remove the anchor stitches.

C to D. Finally, attach the footpad to the bottom opening of the leg, stitching the pad to the leg all the way around. You may find it helpful to tack the pad in place with stitches at the toe and heel before sewing it in place.

Jointing

Though this method of jointing is very simple, it took two years of trial and error to perfect it and make certain the joints would hold up with use. I cut the disks from plastic margarine tub lids with a standard hole punch. You can try other types of plastic, but whatever you use must be flexible, not rigid or brittle. Each fully jointed bear requires ten disks: two for each joint.

The jointing wires are jewelry headpins. These can be found at most craft and hobby stores. Each bear uses five headpins: one for each joint. If faced with a choice of head sizes at the store, choose

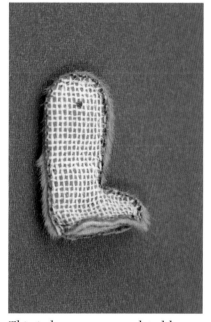

This is how your completed leg should look before turning.

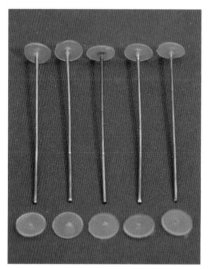

A complete set of joints consists of five headpins and ten plastic disks. Use a standard size paper punch to cut the disks from a plastic material, such as magarine tub lids.

the larger heads. The length of the headpin isn't important, as you will cut most of it off during the jointing process. I like to keep the snipped wires to use in making accessories, such as tiny eyeglasses.

Punch your disks, then use a darning needle to make a hole in the center of each. Thread one disk onto each of five headpins.

Turn all the pieces right-side out. Now that you have added pads to the bear's arms, you have a definite right and left arm. The pads should be on the bear's inner arm. The inner arms have a joint marking to indicate where you mount the joint. The body has joint markings for the arms and legs.

Both legs are identical, so it doesn't really matter which one goes where. The legs have joint markings on each side of both pieces, so no matter on which side you mount the joint, it will be positioned appropriately. Don't forget to create a right and a left leg, though!

To mount the arm and leg joints, simply poke the jointing wire (with the disk attached) through the arm or leg from the inside at the joint mark. You may find it helpful to partially turn the top of the arm or leg inside out to locate the joint marking.

To joint the head, insert the jointing disk into the neck opening. Use a running stitch to gather the neck opening around the joint wire. Try to keep the wire centered in the head so your bear won't look lopsided. Once you are certain the head is securely closed around the jointing wire, tie a knot and bury your thread.

To complete the jointing process, you must attach the arms, legs and head to the body. Starting with a leg, run the jointing wire through the outside of the body at the appropriate spot, coming out at the joint marking inside the body. Thread a disk onto the wire inside the body and pull the wire firmly to seat the disk. Using your sidecutters, snip the wire to about ¼" (6mm). Use your hemostats to roll the end of the wire into a loop. It is the tension of the loop against

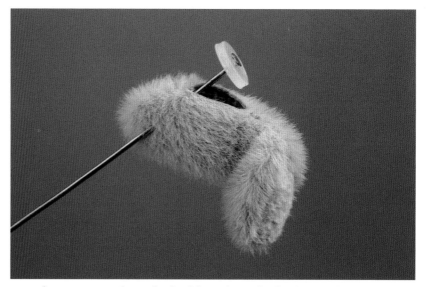

Run the joint wire through the fabric from the backing side at the joint markings. Thread it through one of the holes in the backing material as close to the center of the joint marking dot as possible.

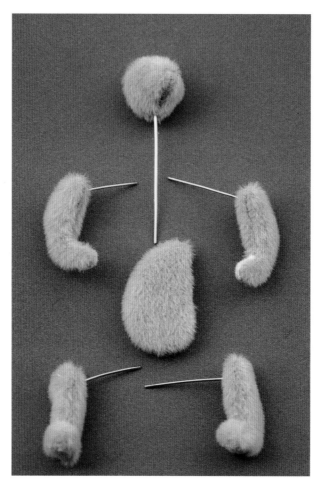

You can joint your bear more efficiently if you start by inserting the joints in the head and all four limbs and then proceeding to the actual jointing procedure.

Work the joint wire through the body fabric from the fur side, coming out at the joint marking dot. Thread a plastic disk onto the joint wire, pushing it firmly against the disk that is in the limb. Make sure the fabric isn't bunched up between the disks.

Use your sidecutters to snip the joint wire to about ¼" (about 6mm) or less. Everyone's technique for curling the joint wire is different. As you joint more bears, you will learn how much wire you need for your particular style.

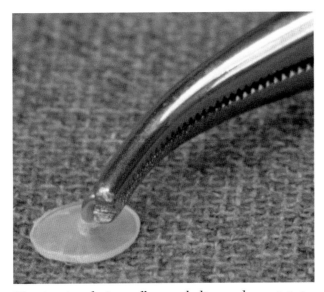

Use tiny, jeweler's needle-nosed pliers or hemostats to curl the wire into a loop.

The completed joint. (This is inside the bear's body.)

the disk that provides for a nice, tight joint. A good test for your joints is to try to move the arm or leg at this point. If it moves easily, your joint isn't snug enough. Keep in mind that the joints will loosen when you stuff your bear. Attach the other leg and both of the arms. The illustrations show the jointing process on a flat piece of fabric so you can see it more clearly.

Attaching the head to the body is accomplished in the same way as the arms and legs. The main difference is that there is no marking on the body to show where the head should go. The positioning of the head is governed by personal taste, your stuffing style and other factors. I like to hold the body and head sideways and move the pieces back and forth to find the best position for the head. Once you determine the perfect position for the head, thread the jointing wire through the body at that point, right on the seam.

Hold the head up to the body and choose the spot where you would like to mount the head. Work the head's jointing wire carefully through the stitches, right on the seam.

Carefully work the wire in between your stitches.

Slide a disk onto the jointing wire, snip it to ¼″ (6mm) and curl it as you did with the arms and legs. When curling the wire for the head joint, it is preferable to curl from front to back or back to front (of the head), as opposed to curling it from left to right. Curling from left to right or vice versa may give you a tilted or lopsided head. Though this can be an endearing trait, in many cases it simply looks like sloppy work.

Stuffing

Stuff the body of your bear firmly, especially around the joints. Stitch up the back seam. Stuff the legs next, followed by the arms, again stuffing very firmly around the joints. Close the seams. Brush all the seams thoroughly.

Eyes

The eyes are mounted much the same as they were in previous projects. The main difference is that instead of working through the neck opening, you work from the back of the neck. This serves an additional purpose, as it sculpts the head, accentuating the hump on the bear's back. Section one of this book covers the process in detail.

Insert your double-threaded needle into the left side of the back of the bear's neck. Leave a long tail of thread at the insertion point. Bring the needle out at the point where his right eye will be. Run the needle through a 2mm eye bead. Reinsert the needle about ¹⁄₃₂″ (less than 1mm) from your exit point. Bring the needle out near your starting point at the back of the neck. Tie a half-knot, using the two ends of your thread. Pull tightly. Repeat the process for the left eye, starting your thread at the right side of the back of the bear's neck.

Tighten up your half-knot for each eye, making certain both eyes are pulled into the head an equal distance. When satisfied with the look you have achieved, tie another half-knot with each set of threads. Bury the thread tails in the head.

Finishing Touches

Stitch your bear's nose and mouth, then attach his ears. Don't forget to trim any stray hairs from around his eyes and mouth! You might want to stitch three or four tiny claws on each paw and foot. Tie a big bow around his neck and give him a tiny hug.

INTERMISSION

*I*f you have been completing these projects in order, congratulate yourself! You have learned all the basics of miniature bearmaking! The remaining projects in this book are "special effects"—tips, techniques and motivators to move you along the road to becoming a teddy bear designer and artist.

So take a deep breath, gather your tools and supplies and follow me into a world where teddy bears say "no-no," Santa is a bruin and bears turn into bunnies!

Jester Bear

This colorful project introduces simple incorporated clothing techniques. I also provide instructions for making a poupard for the teddy to carry!

MATERIALS

- small pieces of upholstery fabric in three colors:
    - a natural bear color, such as tan or white
    - two different, complementary colors or patterns
- small piece of synthetic suede for pads
- ribbon for collar
- various other trims of your choosing
- no. 12 quilting needle
- darning needle
- cotton batting or polyester fiberfill
- very fine, clear nylon thread *or*
- thread that matches your fabric
- black, fine point permanent marker
- two 2mm (or smaller) black beads
- fine thread for nose and mouth
- craft glue
- ten ¼" or 6mm plastic disks and ten headpins (for joints)

JESTER ▶
These pieces should be cut from the fabric you have designated as Color 1.
Arrow indicates direction of nap
BODY—*Cut one.*
LEG—*Cut one of each.*
INNER ARM—*Cut one.*
OUTER ARM—*Cut one.*

Pattern and Layout

Dressed teddy bears are darling, but effectively dressing a miniature bear is difficult. Such a small bear doesn't carry the added bulk of clothing very gracefully. It also seems a shame to cover up the shape of a well-designed bear. One way around this dilemma is to incorporate the clothing into the bear's design. In other words, the clothing replaces, not covers, the bear's body parts.

The Jester's head is crafted from fabric that is a typical teddy bear color. The rest of the bear is created from two different colors that go nicely together. This gives the illusion that the teddy is wearing a neck-to-toe outfit. The body is composed of both colors: the left side of the body is one color, and the right side is the other. One arm and leg are made from each color of fabric. These are jointed to the side of the body that doesn't match their color.

Because of the color layout of this project, it is important to follow the color key on the pattern for laying out the pieces. As you select the two complementary col-

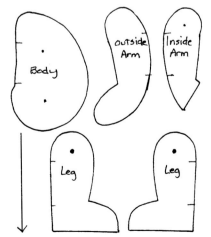

ors you will use for the body parts, assign the number 1 to one color and the number 2 to the other. The pattern is offered in three sections to indicate which color number the pieces should be cut from.

Trace and cut out all the pattern pieces.

Sewing

Stitch all the bear's pattern pieces as instructed in the previous projects. Refer back to project five if necessary for inserting the paw and footpads. You should stuff the head at this point, but do not stitch the neck area closed. The eyes, nose, mouth and ears will be added after jointing.

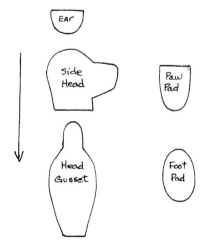

▲
These pieces should be cut from neutral, bear-like colors
Arrow indicates direction of nap
SIDE HEAD—*Cut two. (Trace one, reverse, trace second.)*
EAR—*Cut four.*
HEAD GUSSET—*Cut one.*
PAWPAD—*Cut two from synthetic suede.*
FOOTPAD—*Cut two from synthetic suede.*

*These pieces should be cut
from the fabric you have
designated as Color 2.
Arrow indicates direction of nap*
BODY—*Cut one.*
LEG—*Cut one of each.*
INNER ARM—*Cut one.*
OUTER ARM—*Cut one.*

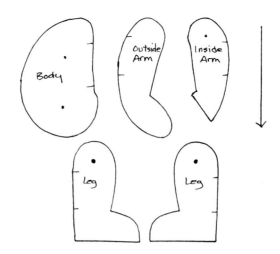

Jointing

Turn all the pieces right-side out.
Insert your joints in the arms, legs
and head. Refer to project five
(pages 55-58) if needed.

Joint the legs, arms and head
to the body, in order. Save the
excess wires you cut from the
headpins. We will use one of them
in the creation of the poupard.

Completing
Construction

Stuff the body of your bear firmly,
especially around the joints. Stitch
up the back seam. Stuff the legs
next, followed by the arms, again
stuffing very firmly around the
joints. Close the seams and brush
them thoroughly.

Mount and seat the Jester's
eyes. Refer to page 58 if necessary. Stitch your bear's nose and
mouth. Use colorful thread if you
wish! Attach your bear's ears.

Ruffles and
Flourishes

Jester bears are a lot of fun to do,
and a great deal of the fun is in
the decorating! You may wish to
keep your Jester simple, but you
can also make him as elaborate as
you like. I use ruffled collars on
a lot of projects, not just Jesters.

The length of ribbon needed
for a ruffled collar is determined
by how tight you want the ruffle
to be. The tighter the ruffle, the
more ribbon it will take. Gather
the ribbon with a running stitch
along one edge of the ribbon. If
you prefer a collar that isn't quite
so wide, start with more narrow

ribbon or fold wide ribbon in
half lengthwise. Run your gathering stitch along the folded edge.
Besides making the collar more
narrow, this technique makes a
double ruffle which looks nice.

When you've gathered enough
ribbon to make a collar that pleases
you, fit it around your bear's neck.
Tie the gathering threads at the
back of the neck. Carefully cut the
ribbon. Use a darning needle to
apply a small amount of craft glue
to the cut ends of the ribbon to
prevent fraying.

I have stitched tiny thread bows
to the front of my bear's outfit.
He still seems to need a little
something, so let's add poupard!

*Did you follow
the color layout
for the project?
Your bear's
limbs should
attach on the
side of the body
that is the con-
trasting color.*

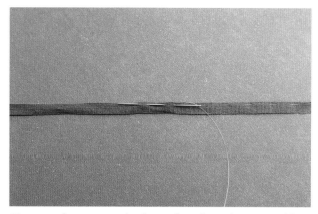

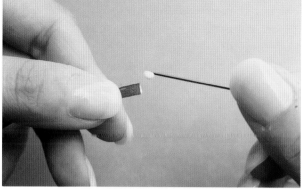

Use a gathering stitch along the edge of pretty ribbon to create a ruffle for your Jester.

Apply glue to the cut edges of ribbon to prevent fraying.

MAKING A POUPARD

As a charming option, you can make this tiny poupard for your Jester to hold. Poupards, marottes and folies were popular toys in the eighteenth and nineteenth centuries, and are simply fancy rattles. The original versions were doll heads mounted on a stick or handle. Clothing or decoration concealed a musical movement or squeaker that was activated by swinging, turning or pressing the toy.

Stitch the head together as you did the Jester's. Turn right-side out. Stuff firmly, but do not close the neck opening. Mount and seat the seed bead eyes through the neck opening. Thread the disk onto the headpin and insert it in the head opening. You may need to trim the disk to fit.

The materials list specifies a straight headpin because it serves as the handle of the poupard. When a headpin is used as a joint, it is snipped and concealed, so it doesn't matter if it is straight.

Gather the neck opening around the headpin with a running stitch. Tie a knot and bury your thread. Stitch your bear's

> ### MATERIALS
> - small piece of upholstery fabric
> - no. 12 quilting needle
> - very fine, clear nylon thread *or*
> - thread that matches your fabric
> - thread for nose in any color you choose
> - black, fine point permanent marker
> - craft glue
> - cotton batting or polyester fiberfill
> - two very small, black seed beads
> - headpin (as straight as possible)
> - one ¼" or 6mm plastic disk
> - small goldtone beads (3-5mm)
> - tiny bells (optional)
> - various trim of your choosing

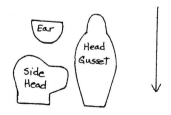

POUPARD
Arrow indicates direction of nap
SIDE HEAD—*Cut two. (Trace one, reverse, trace second.)*

EAR—*Cut four.*
HEAD GUSSET—*Cut one.*

nose and mouth, possibly using the same thread you used for the Jester. Stitch the ears and attach to the head.

Hold the poupard up to the Jester and, determining the appropriate length for the handle, cut the headpin to the right length.

Decorate your poupard any way you wish. Add ruffles and ribbons, or add tiny bells to the mix. You can add blush to the cheeks, too.

A nice finishing touch is to add a bead at the bottom of the handle. Simply dip the end of the headpin in craft glue, then insert it in the hole of a goldtone bead. Set aside until the glue dries.

When the poupard is finished, your can either stitch or tie it to the Jester's paw or let him hold it in the crook of his arm.

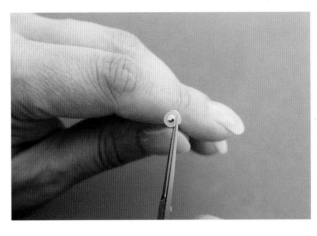

Trim the plastic disk so that it fits inside the neck opening.

Cut the handle of the poupard to an appropriate length. Hold the poupard up to your Jester to help you decide what length would be appealing.

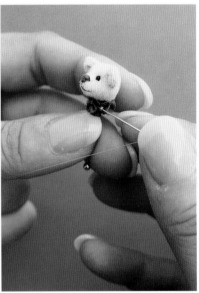

Have fun decorating your poupard!

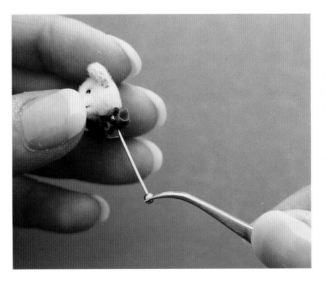

Add a bead to the bottom of the poupard handle for a nice, finished look.

Panda

Although pandas are not true bears, they are welcomed into the collections of the vast majority of teddy bear collectors with open arms. They radiate a special charm that makes them irresistible to both artists and collectors. Pandas have unique black and white coloring which sets them apart from other "bears," but there are other differences as well. Incorporating these differences into your design will make your work more realistic and appealing.

MATERIALS

- small pieces of upholstery fabric (black and ecru)
- small piece of synthetic suede for pads
- no. 12 quilting needle
- very fine, clear nylon thread *or*
- thread that matches your fabric
- black thread for nose
- black, fine point permanent marker
- trim of your choice
- two 2mm (or smaller) black beads
- ten ¼" or 6mm plastic disks for joints
- five headpins for joints
- cotton batting or polyester fiberfill

Fabric Selection

When observing the coloration of real pandas, you will notice that their white fur isn't a pure white, but more of an ecru color. I find that using off-white as opposed to snow-white fur gives my pandas a warm look that I like very much. Of course, you can use any colors you wish! Many artists use incredibly colored fabrics to create delightful pandas that are fanciful rather than realistic.

Layout

After selecting the fabrics you will be using, lay out the pattern on the fabric. The pattern, as shown, will make a 3" (about 7cm) bear.

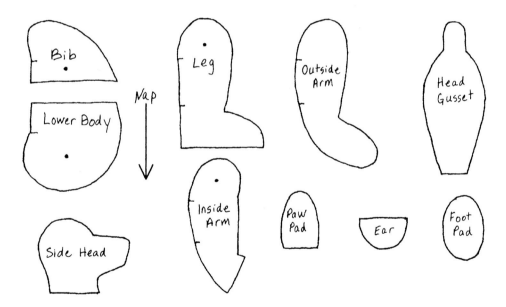

PANDA

Arrow indicates direction of nap

BIB—*Cut two. (Trace one, reverse, trace second.)*

LOWER BODY—*Cut two. (Trace one, reverse, trace second.)*

LEG—*Cut four. (Trace two, reverse, trace two more.)*

SIDE HEAD—*Cut two. (Trace one, reverse, trace second.)*

INNER ARM—*Cut two. (Trace one, reverse, trace second.)*

OUTER ARM—*Cut two. (Trace one, reverse, trace second.)*

PAWPAD—*Cut two.*

EAR—*Cut four.*

HEAD GUSSET—*Cut one.*

FOOTPAD—*Cut two.*

Live pandas have black ears, eye rings, arms and legs. The top portion of their body, the bib, is black as well. The only white areas are the head and the bottom part of the body. I use black for the paw-pads, although that makes it difficult to see the stitches as I am working. A light colored pad that matches the color of the head and lower body works nicely, too, and makes it easier to keep a close watch on your stitching. Lay out your pattern pieces, making certain to transfer all the markings.

Construction

After cutting out the pieces, match a bib with its corresponding body-bottom. Stitch the two pieces together along the imaginary line that would be the bear's waist. Do the same with the other two body pieces. Sew the left side and right side of the bear together. Sew the remaining parts of the bear.

When your pieces are all sewn, join the arms and legs to the body using the traditional jointing techniques learned in project five (see pages 55-58). Stuff the head, and join it to the body using the same technique. Read through all the instructions given here, first!

Shaping the Head

One distinguishing characteristic of a panda is the shape of its head. It is narrower at the top where the small ears are daintily perched. To create this effect in the pandas I make, I use the stitches that anchor the eyes to sculpt the head.

Insert your double-threaded needle into the area where your panda's left ear will be. Leave a long tail of thread at the insertion point. Bring the needle out at the point where his right eye will be. Run your needle through your 2mm eye bead. Reinsert the needle about $1/32''$ (less than 1mm) from your exit point. Bring the needle out at the point where your panda's left ear will be, about $1/32''$ (less than 1mm) from your starting point. Tie a half-knot, using the two ends of your thread. Pull tightly. Repeat the process for the left eye, starting your thread at the point where your bear's right ear will be.

Tighten up your half-knot for each eye, making certain both eyes are pulled into the head an equal distance. When satisfied with the look you have achieved, tie another half-knot with each set of threads. Bury the thread tails in the head.

By anchoring the eyes to the corners of the head, you can create a sculptured effect that will give your panda a more realistic look.

Stuffing

Stuff your bear as usual, paying special attention to the tummy area. Pandas have voracious appetites, and you don't want yours to look hungry! Stitch your panda's nose and mouth using fine black thread. Sew and attach the ears, using the sculpted indentations in the head as your placement guide.

Eye Patches

Some artists use piecing techniques to create the eye patches on their pandas. This works wonderfully for larger bears, but when making a miniature panda, the piecing technique simply adds too much bulk. I create the patches with careful use of a fine-tip permanent marker. I use the Pigma Micron 005 marker for this. You need an ink that will dry quickly and will not bleed.

The technique that works best for me is to use a dabbing motion as opposed to a drawing motion. Starting right at the spot where you have mounted your panda's eye, press the pen tip onto the fabric and lift straight off. Press the pen onto the fabric again, right next to your first mark. Work your way out from the eye. I like to work a little bit on one eye, then work a little on the other. Do your best to make patches that match one another. No matter what shape the patches are, if they match, they will look great. If they are uneven, the whole bear will look lopsided.

Use a dabbing motion to apply the pigment to the eye area. Begin as close to the eye bead as possible.

Work your way outward from the bead. Be conservative. You can always add more pigment later, but once it's applied, it's impossible to remove.

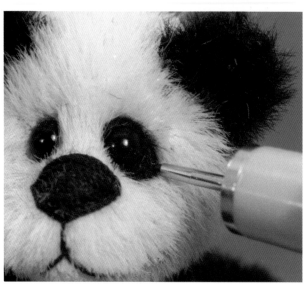

The majority of the pigment should be applied beneath the eye area toward the cheek.

As you apply the pigment, view your bear from several angles to make certain you are getting the look you want.

The final shape of the eye patch is a matter of personal preference. I usually shape the patch like an inverted teardrop, but this photo shows a more rounded patch.

Trim

Traditional pandas look great with just a simple red bow, but you can add all sorts of interesting trims to create a more elaborate piece. Panda clowns, angels and Santas are just a few options. How about creating miniature bamboo from clay for him to hold? By shrinking or enlarging your pattern, you can make pandas in various sizes and assemble an entire family!

Here is my completed panda with satin trim and goldtone heart. The pattern is the same, but this one stands only 2″ (about 5cm) tall.

Santa Bear

The Santa Bear project incorporates more elaborate piecing techniques which will give your designs a very polished appearance. The addition of fur-colored paws, applied cuffs and built-in boots are little touches that can set your work apart. The hat and toy sack are optional, as is the very tiny bear that goes in the sack.

MATERIALS

- small pieces of upholstery fabric in three colors: tan, red and black
- small piece of white (6″ × ¼″ or 15cm × 6mm), longer-napped upholstery fabric for cuffs
- synthetic suede in a neutral color for pawpads
- black synthetic suede or upholstery fabric for boot/footpads and belt
- two 2mm (or smaller) black onyx beads
- small goldtone beads
- no. 12 quilting needle
- darning needle
- very fine, clear nylon thread *or*
- thread that matches your fabric
- brown or black thread for nose and mouth
- small belt buckle or headpin wire
- craft glue
- ten ¼″ or 6mm plastic disks and ten headpins (for joints)

Pattern and Layout

Because of the color layout of this project, it is important to follow the color key on the pattern for laying out the pieces. The pattern is marked to indicate which fabric each piece should be cut from. Trace the pattern pieces onto the appropriate fabrics as indicated.

The only real differences in the basic pattern for this project are the upper paws and the boots. The upper paws are applied in exactly the same manner as the pawpads. The boots are created by dividing the leg just above the ankle and replacing the foot area with black upholstery fabric or synthetic suede. You may wish to use a quilter's pencil or white opaque pen to trace onto the black synthetic suede.

SANTA BEAR
Arrow indicates direction of nap
BODY—*Cut two (red). (Trace one, reverse, trace second.)*
LEG—*Cut four (red). (Trace two, reverse, trace two more.)*
BOOT—*Cut four (black). (Trace two, reverse, trace two more.)*
SIDE HEAD—*Cut two (tan). (Trace one, reverse, trace second.)*
INNER ARM—*Cut two (red). (Trace one, reverse, trace second.)*
OUTER ARM (same pattern piece as inner arm)—*Cut two (red). (Trace one, reverse, trace second.)*
UPPER PAW/PAWPAD—*Cut two (tan), cut two (synthetic suede).*
EAR—*Cut four (tan).*
HEAD GUSSET—*Cut one (tan).*
FOOTPAD—*Cut two (black).*
HAT—*Cut one (red).*
BELT—*Cut one (black synthetic suede).*

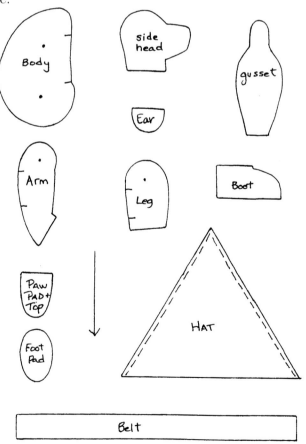

Sewing

Stitch the bear's head and body as instructed in previous projects. Stitch the pawpads to a right and a left arm piece, then stitch the upper paw to the two remaining arm pieces. Note that because of the addition of an upper paw, all four arm pieces are short. Make certain that you end up with a right and left arm piece with a pawpad attached, and a right and left arm with an upper paw. Stitch each arm together using a "pawpad arm" and an "upper paw arm" to create a completed arm.

You will notice that the leg pieces have a flatter side (the back) and a more rounded side (the front). Sew a boot to each leg piece, being careful to align the pieces so that the toe of the boot matches up with the front of the leg. The heel should line up with the flat or back side of the leg. Stitch the legs together as in previous projects, remembering to leave an opening in the back for turning.

Insert the footpads as in previous projects. Working with black synthetic suede is not easy, as it is difficult to see your stitches. Working under a very bright light helps a great deal.

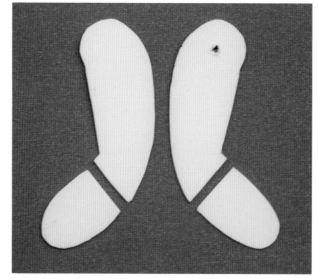

Each arm is constructed from four pieces: the outer arm, the inner arm, the upper paw and the pawpad.

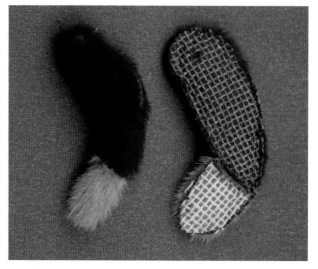

Stitch the upper pads and pawpads to the appropriate arm pieces. Be sure to end up with a left arm and a right arm! Here is a view of two arms: one before turning and one after.

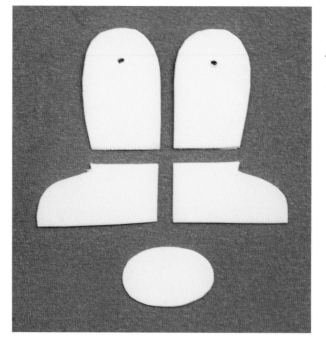

Each of Santa's legs consists of five pieces: two legs, two boots and a footpad.

Stitch each of the boots to a leg piece, matching up the heel of the boot with the flatter side of the leg. Sew the left and right sides of each leg together. Insert and stitch the footpad as instructed in previous projects.

Your completed leg should look like this after turning.

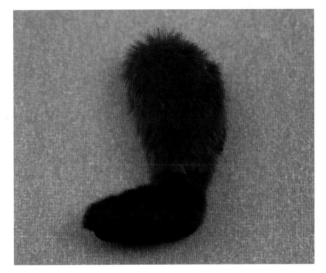

Joint your Santa, making certain that the pawpads face toward his body.

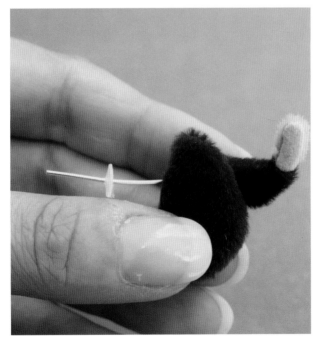

Jointing

Turn all the pieces right-side out. Insert joints in the arms and legs. Refer to project five (pages 55-58) if needed. Stuff the head and insert the joint. Use a running stitch to gather the neck around the jointing wire.

Joint the legs, arms and head to the body, in that order. Save the excess wire that you cut from the headpins if you need to create a belt buckle. Make sure the synthetic suede side of the arms face towards the body.

Completing Construction

Stuff the body of your bear firmly, especially around the joints. Stitch up the back seam. Stuff the legs next, followed by the arms, again stuffing very firmly around the joints. Close the seams. Brush all the seams thoroughly.

Mount and seat the eyes. Again, refer to project five if necessary. Stitch your bear's nose and mouth. Sew and attach the bear's ears.

Fold the strip of cuff fabric in half lengthwise and stitch along the long edge. This strip is too narrow to turn, so stitch it right-side out. This photo shows a small segment of cuff being stitched.

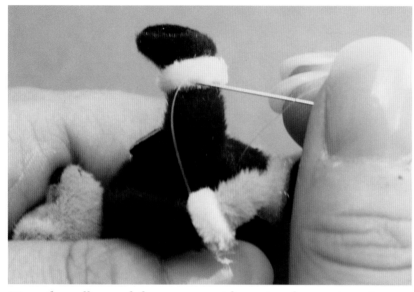

Wrap the cuff around the area you wish to trim, then cut it to the appropriate length. Sew the cuff to the body using either a whipstitch along the edges or a running stitch down the middle.

Add a cuff to the hat, if desired.

Finishing Touches

Although he has incorporated clothing, your Santa Bear still needs some special touches to be complete. You can create the cuffs simply by cutting strips of longer white fur to fit around both wrists and ankles and sewing or gluing them in place. I prefer a slightly more complicated process, and believe it is well worth the added effort.

Use the 6″ × ¼″ (15cm × 6mm) strip of longer white fabric to create the cuffs. Fold the fabric lengthwise, fur sides out, and stitch along the long edge. This creates a tube. Cut cuffs to length from this tube and stitch them to each wrist and ankle. Depending upon the length of the pile, you may wish to trim the fur on the cuffs.

Cut a hat from red fur using the pattern provided. Fold fur sides with dotted lines together and stitch. No two heads are stitched or stuffed alike, so you may need to adjust the size of the hat to fit your bear's head. You may wish to add a bit of stuffing inside the hat to give it more definition. Use a needle or two to hold the hat in place while you whipstitch it to the head. Use the remaining cuff material to trim the bottom edge of the hat.

It may seem silly to go to all the trouble of putting an ear in place under the hat, but it isn't! Every time I sell a bear that is wearing a hat, the new owner's first question is, "Does he have an ear under there?" Taking shortcuts in your bearmaking is not recommended.

You may leave the hat as-is, or you can fold the tip over and stitch it in place. I feel this gives more of a "Santa look" than leaving it standing up. You can also attach a bell, bead or other trim to the tip of the hat.

To create the belt, simply cut a strip of black synthetic suede to fit the buckle you will be using. The belt pattern piece shows the size piece I used for the bear shown. Wrap the belt around the bear's middle, threading the synthetic suede through the buckle. You can tack the belt in place with a few stitches or a bit of craft glue, if you wish. Cut the tail-end of the belt in a pleasing shape, and use a drop of glue to hold it flat against the belt.

If you aren't able to find an appropriately sized buckle, create one from one of the headpin wires. You can find tiny buckles and many other wonderful accessories at miniature (dollhouse) shows that are held across the country year-round.

Attach the belt to the bear's waist with a few stitches or a tiny bit of craft glue.

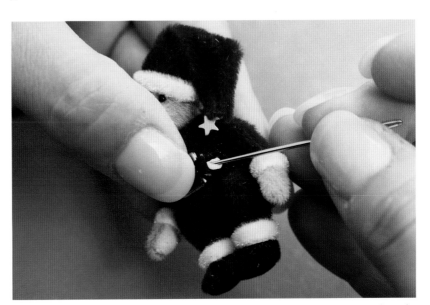

After trimming the tail of the belt, hold it in place with a drop of craft glue.

If you are unable to find a tiny, premade buckle such as the one on the left, you can craft a buckle similar to the one on the right from leftover joint wire.

MAKING THE TOY SACK AND TINY BEAR

THE COMPLETED TOY SACK

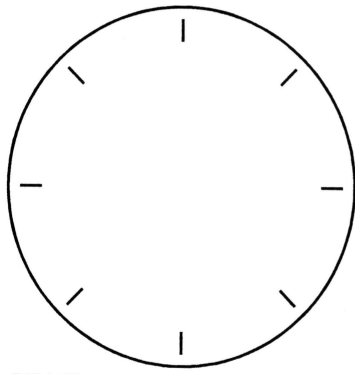

TOY SACK
Cut one from red or black synthetic suede.

The Toy Sack

Trace and cut the sack from red synthetic suede using the pattern provided. Around the outer edge of the fabric circle, cut small slits perpendicular to the edge of the fabric. Space them about ½″ (1¼cm) apart. Weave one piece of drawstring cording through the slits all the way around the edge of the fabric. Tie the ends of the cord together. Do the same with a second piece of cording, but this time start on the opposite side of the sack.

Tiny Teddy Bear

You can fill the toy sack with all sorts of miniature toys, including this tiny bear. This little fellow is created entirely of synthetic suede and is string jointed. Trace, cut and stitch him together as in previous projects, and turn the pieces right-side out. Stuff the head, then add the eyes and ears. Stitch the nose and mouth. Stuff and joint the remaining pieces, referring to the string jointing techniques in project two if necessary. Do not brush his seams. Tie a bow around his neck or decorate him any way you wish. Well-executed bears of this size never fail to elicit "oohs" and "aahs" wherever they appear.

MATERIALS

- red or black synthetic suede for Toy Sack
- cording of your choice for drawstring
- synthetic suede in two colors for the tiny bear
- other trims and toys of your choosing
- no. 12 quilting needle
- very fine, clear nylon thread *or*
- thread that matches your fabric
- black or brown thread for nose and mouth
- two very small, seed beads for eyes
- other trim of your choosing

The completed toy sack bear is sure to amaze people, especially when they discover it is jointed.

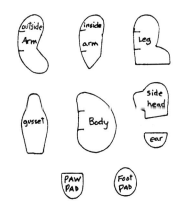

TINY TOY SACK BEAR

Note: Synthetic suede doesn't have a nap, so there is no arrow indicating a nap direction for this pattern. Cut the paw and footpads from a lighter shade of synthetic suede than the rest of the bear.

BODY—*Cut two. (Trace one, reverse, trace second.)*
LEG—*Cut four. (Trace two, reverse, trace two more.)*
SIDE HEAD—*Cut two. (Trace one, reverse, trace second.)*
INNER ARM—*Cut two. (Trace one, reverse, trace second.)*
OUTER ARM—*Cut two. (Trace one, reverse, trace second.)*
PAWPAD—*Cut two.*
EAR—*Cut four.*
HEAD GUSSET—*Cut one.*
FOOTPAD—*Cut two.*

The time and effort needed to create a project like this is well worth the effort when you see the end result.

No-no Bear

No-no bears are fascinating even when they are a foot tall, but they become amazing when they are miniaturized. It's such fun to watch peoples' faces light up when you demonstrate this little bear's talents. The bear has a lever on its back that causes his head to move left and right.

This project also introduces another approach to design: The four-piece body and one-piece arms and legs are reminiscent of vintage Steiff patterns. The four-piece body allows you to add more shape and contours to your design.

Pattern and Layout

In addition to the new body, arm and leg design, this bear also has a tail. The direction of the nap for the tail doesn't matter much, as the tail is so small. If you adapt this idea to a larger bear, you may wish to experiment with nap direction.

Trace and cut out all the pattern pieces, paying careful attention to the direction of the nap.

Sewing

The most difficult aspect of working with a four-piece body is remembering which piece goes where. I have found that the best way to handle this is to mark the pieces well, so that there is no question of which piece is which. Stitch the left front (LF) piece to the left back (LB) piece. Do the same for the front and back pieces for the right side of the body (RF and RB). That will give you a left body and right body to sew together, just as you have done in previous projects. Don't forget to leave an opening in the back for turning and stuffing!

The arms and legs are relatively

MATERIALS

- small piece of upholstery fabric
- small piece of synthetic suede for pads
- trim of your choosing
- no. 12 quilting needle
- darning needle
- very fine, clear nylon thread *or*
- thread that matches your fabric
- two 2mm (or smaller) black beads
- black or brown thread for nose and mouth
- black, fine point permanent marker
- craft glue or Super Glue brand glue
- ten ¼″ or 6mm plastic disks and ten headpins (for joints)

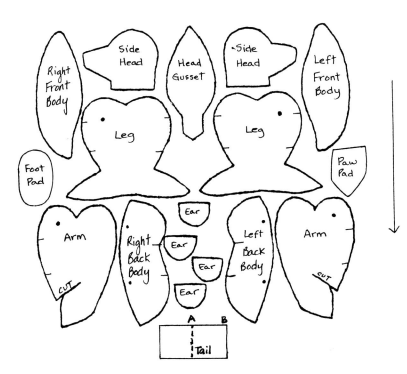

NO-NO BEAR
Arrow indicates direction of nap. Cut one of each pattern piece as shown, except paw and footpads:
RIGHT FRONT BODY
LEFT FRONT BODY
RIGHT BACK BODY
LEFT BACK BODY
LEGS
ARMS
SIDE HEADS
HEAD GUSSET
EARS
TAIL
PAWPAD—*Cut two from synthethic suede. (Trace one, reverse, trace second.)*
FOOTPAD—*Cut two from synthetic suede.*

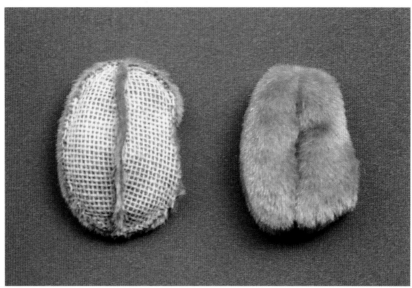

Mark the body pieces clearly to help you keep them organized.

Stitch the front piece to the back piece for both the left and right sides of the body.

simple. For the arms, stitch the pawpad to the short side of the arm. Note that the pawpad has a definite direction to it unlike the pads in previous projects. You need to position the pad so that it is a mirror image of the fur portion of the paw on the arm. When you fold the arm over, right sides together, the arms and paws should align. Stitch around the top edge of the arm. Leave an opening in the back of the arm for turning, then stitch the rest of the seam.

Stitch the top, rounded edge of the legs, leaving a gap in the front. Then stitch from the ankle to the toe. Insert the footpad as usual.

The tail is stitched right before it is attached to the body. Stuff the head at this point, but do not stitch the neck area closed. The eyes, nose, mouth and ears will be added after jointing.

Stitch the left side of the body to the right, leaving an opening in the back for turning and stuffing. This view from the top of the body shows how the four seams should align.

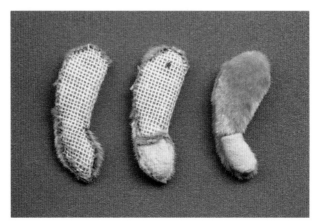

This photo shows both sides of the arm after stitching and the completed, turned arm.

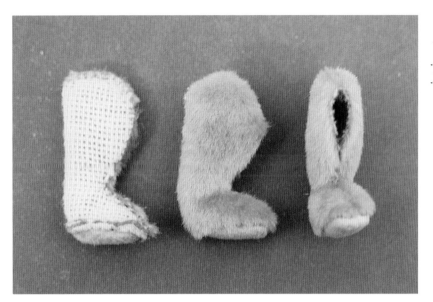

Here is a stitched leg before and after turning. Note that the opening for turning and stuffing is in the front of the limb.

Jointing

Turn all the pieces right-side out. Insert your joints in the arms and legs. Refer to project five, pages 55-58, if needed. Joint the legs and arms to the body, in that order.

It is the head joint wire that makes the no-no mechanism. Instead of snipping the head joint wire off, it is run through the body and out at the tail area. The protruding wire is then cut to an appropriate length, bent into a loop and covered with fabric. The disk that is mounted inside the head must be attached so that when you move the tail, the entire head will move, not just the joint wire. To accomplish this, dip the jointing disk into craft glue or Super Glue brand glue. I prefer Super Glue, as it makes the bottom of the head very firm and anchors the disk solidly with no "give." Insert the jointing disk into the neck opening. Use a running stitch to gather the neck opening around the joint wire. Try to keep the wire centered in the head so your bear won't look lopsided. Once you are certain the head is securely closed around the jointing wire, tie a knot and bury your thread. Set the head aside and let the glue set.

When the glue inside your bear's head has set completely, insert the joint wire into the body at a pleasing point. Slide the second disk on the wire and push it up firmly against the inside surface of the body. Do not cut the joint wire! Run the wire through the body, coming out at the spot where you wish the tail to be. This mechanism will be completed after the bear is completely stuffed.

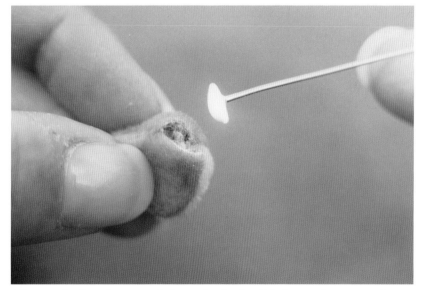

Glue applied to the joint disk inside the head helps anchor it in place. This prevents slippage when the no-no mechanism is used. Insert the glue-laden joint into the head.

Completing Construction

Stuff the body of your bear firmly, especially around the joints. The no-no wire that is routed through the body makes stuffing a bit tricky, but do your best to keep the majority of the wire buried in the stuffing. Stitch up the back seam. Stuff the legs next, followed by the arms, again stuffing very firmly around the joints. Close the seams. Brush all the seams thoroughly.

Mount and seat the bear's eyes. Again, refer to project five if necessary. Stitch your bear's nose and mouth. Stitch the ears to his head.

Completing the Mechanism

Fold the tail covering on the dotted line and stitch around three edges from point A to point B. Leave one of the short sides open for turning. This creates a pocket to slip over the tail wire. After stitching, tie a knot, but do not cut your thread. You will use the thread to stitch the tail to the body.

Pull the tail wire firmly. Make sure the bear's head is facing forward and is resting snugly against the body. Snip the wire to a length of about ¼" (about 6mm). Use small pliers or hemostats to loop the wire into a flattened oval shape. This serves two purposes: First, it prevents the tail wire from migrating back into the body. Second, it provides a larger surface to grip when activating the mechanism.

Turn the fabric tail pocket

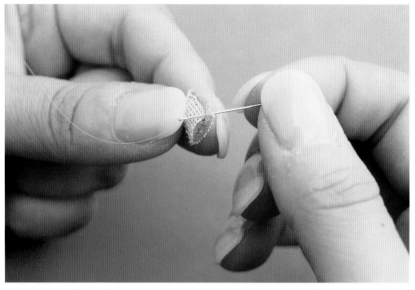

Stitch the tail, making a little pocket to slip over the tail wire. Leave the thread attached for stitching the tail to the body.

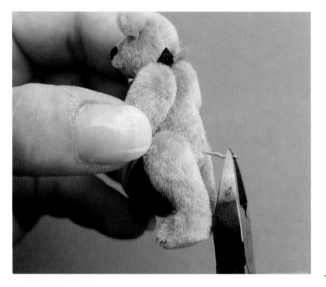

Carefully thread the joint wire between the stitches, directly on the seam. The wire should exit at the spot where the tail will look best. Pull the tail firmly and snip the wire, leaving about ¼" (about 6mm) for bending.

Bend the tail wire into a flattened loop.

right-side out. Use a darning needle to apply a small amount of glue to the inside of the tail pocket. Slip the cover onto the tail wire. Press the tail between your thumb and index finger to mold it to the wire. Use the thread on the tail covering to whipstitch the tail to the body.

Tie a knot and bury your thread in the body. When choosing a bow or collar for no-no bears, you must remember to allow for free head movement. To work the tail mechanism, simply grasp the tail and move it left and right.

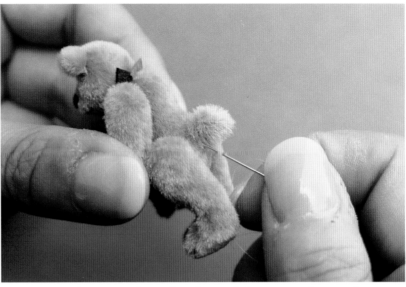

Put a bit of glue inside the tail pocket and slip it over the wire loop. Use a whipstitch to attach the tail to the body.

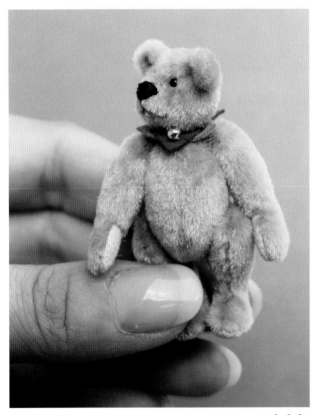

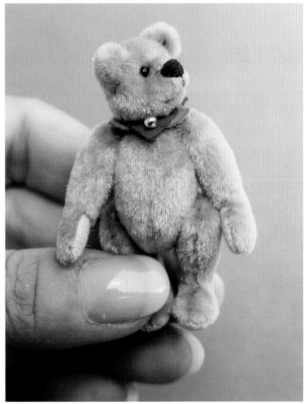

Now your bear can answer any question, provided the answer is no . . . *. . .no!*

Bunny

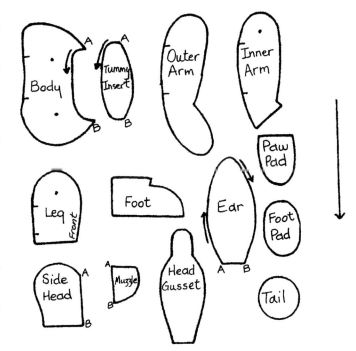

Teddy bears and bunnies go together like toast and jam! Rare is the bear collector who doesn't have at least a few bunnies in his or her collection. With a few minor adjustments, a bear pattern can become a simple bunny pattern. You can take these changes further and alter the arms, legs and body shape. Compare these pattern pieces to the basic bear pattern in project five to see how similar they are!

As you work on this project, pay attention to the correlation between the pattern pieces and the finished, three-dimensional body parts. Understanding the relationship between the two is the first step in being able to create your own designs from scratch.

Two shades of brown or tan should be used for the bunny: a darker color for the main pieces and a lighter color for the tummy, feet, tail and muzzle. In addition to the two fur-type fabrics, synthetic suede in a complementary shade is required for the inside of the ears, the pawpads and the footpads.

Layout and Cutting

The bunny's tummy, feet and muzzle are inset in the same manner as the boots in project eight. The tummy area of each body piece is replaced with a lighter colored fur. The muzzle area of each side head piece is treated in the same manner. The feet are also replaced with the lighter fur. The ears are lined with synthetic suede, and may be wired for poseability if you wish.

BUNNY
Arrow indicates direction of nap.
Cut these pieces from the lighter colored fabric:
TUMMY INSERT—*Cut two. (Trace one, reverse, trace second.)*
FOOT—*Cut four. (Trace two, reverse, trace two more.)*
MUZZLE—*Cut two. (Trace one, reverse, trace second.)*
TAIL—*Cut one.*
Cut these pieces from the darker colored fabric:
BODY—*Cut two. (Trace one, reverse, trace second.)*
LEG—*Cut four. (Trace two,*
reverse, trace two more.)
SIDE HEAD—*Cut two. (Trace one, reverse, trace second.)*
OUTER ARM—*Cut two. (Trace one, reverse, trace second.)*
INNER ARM—*Cut two. (Trace one, reverse, trace second.)*
HEAD GUSSET—*Cut one.*
EAR—*Cut four. (Two from synthetic suede, two from fur.)*
Cut these pieces from synthetic suede:
FOOTPAD—*Cut two from synthetic suede.*
PAWPAD—*Cut two from synthetic suede.*

MATERIALS

- small pieces of upholstery fabric two complementary colors:
  a light color for the tummy, muzzle, feet and tail; a darker color for the rest of the bunny
- synthetic suede for paw and footpads and the inside of the ears
- trim of your choosing
- no. 12 quilting needle
- darning needle
- very fine, clear nylon thread *or*
- thread that matches your fabric
- two 2mm (or smaller) black beads
- pink thread for the nose
- black thread for mouth
- craft glue
- two headpin wires (left over from the joints)
- ten ¼" or 6mm plastic disks and ten headpins (for joints)

Sewing

Stitch the left muzzle to the front of the left side head piece, matching A and B on the pattern pieces. Do the same for the right muzzle and right side head piece. Complete the head assembly as usual.

Stitch the left tummy panel to the left body piece. Do the same for the right tummy panel and body piece. Stitch the left and right body pieces together.

Stitch the feet to the bottom of the legs as instructed in the Santa boots in project eight.

The ears have fur on the back side, and synthetic suede on the front side. Stitch a synthetic suede ear piece to a fur ear piece from A to B, leaving the flat bottom edge open for turning.

Sew the arms and legs together as usual. Stitch the tail just prior to attaching it to the body.

Assembly

Turn all the pieces right-side out. Stuff the head. Joint the head, arms and legs to the body. Mount and seat the eyes. Stuff the body, arms and legs. Stitch the bunny's nose with pink or salmon thread, then use black for the mouth. (Detailed instructions for all steps are given in previous projects.)

To prepare the ears for attachment, put a little glue inside the ear with a darning needle. Press the ear together to give it a tidy appearance. The ears can either be left floppy, or they can be shaped by inserting headpin wire

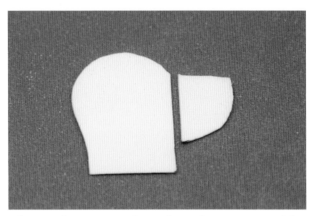

The muzzle piece simply replaces the nose area of the side head piece.

With the muzzle stitched in place, your side head piece will look like this before turning.

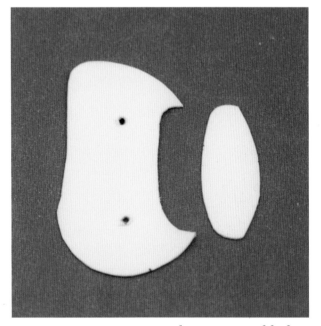

The tummy insert gives your bunny a special look.

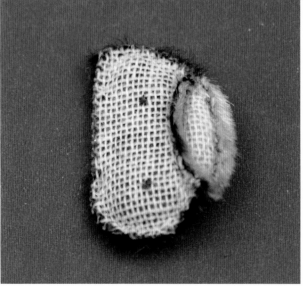

With the tummy inserts in place, your body pieces look like this before turning.

that has been formed to the shape of the ear. Insert the wires after you have added glue to the inside of the ear. Press the ears between your thumb and index finger, or use hemostats to make the fabric conform to the shape of the wires.

Trim the wire inserts so they don't protrude from the ears. Don't simply cut them flush with the raw edge of the fabric. You should snip the wires at least 1⁄16″

(1-2mm) up from the bottom edge of the ear. You don't want the wires to interfere with the stitching of the ears to the head.

Stitch the ears to the head, using the gusset seams as placement guides. Pull those stitches snugly! Arrange and shape the ears as you stitch them to the head. If the ears stick out unattractively, take a few extra stitches at the base of the ear where it is sewn to the head

to "snug" the ears down. (See photos next page.)

You can give your bunny a tail, if you wish. I prefer tail-less bunnies myself.

Prepare the tail for mounting by using a running stitch around the circumference of the fabric circle. Pull the thread snugly, gathering the fabric into a ball-like tail. Stitch the tail to the appropriate spot on the bunny's body.

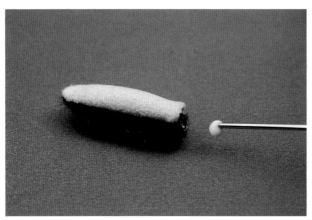

Putting glue inside the ear gives a sculpted look. You can leave the ears floppy or insert shaped wires for a more structured look. In either case, use glue inside the ear.

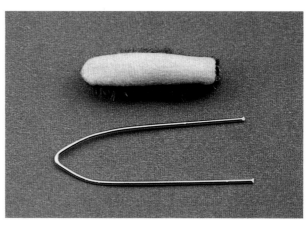

If you wish, you may use shaped wires inside your bunny's ears. Bend headpin wires to an appropriate shape, then slide them into the ear pocket.

Press the ear together to conform the fabric to the ear wires, if you choose to use them, or to the backside of the ear.

Shaping the ears provides appealing definition, making them more realistic and detailed.

Brush all the seams thoroughly. Carefully trim the bunny's face, especially around the eyes. You may add whiskers if you like by simply running white or clear thread through the muzzle with a needle. A cute adornment for bunnies is a carrot necklace. You can find miniature carrots at doll-house shops, or make your own using colored modeling compound. Use a needle or small drill to make a hole near the top of the carrot, then thread it onto a tiny gold cord.

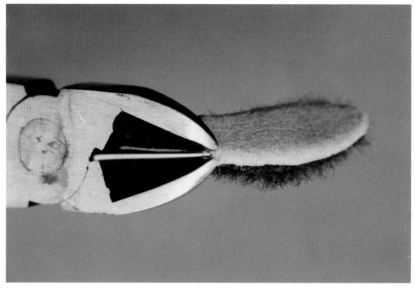

Trim the wire inserts, if necessary, so they don't extend from the ear.

Stitch the ears to the head with a whipstitch.

Bear Business

SELLING WHAT YOU MAKE

So, you have used the tools in this book to perfect your techniques and develop your own style, and now you have piles of little bears all over your house. It's time to find homes for your creations!

The teddy bear world is a wonderful, friendly place. If you make a better bear, as with a mousetrap, the teddy bear world *will* beat a path to your door. Making the jump from teddy bear hobbyist to working artist is something that sneaks up on us. The most memorable step is usually our first sale to someone we don't know. Yet unless people see the bears you make, they won't know how wonderful they are. Here are some tips for getting your business off the ground.

Naming Your Business

For several years, I marketed my bears under the business name "Granny's Locket Bears." This was fine, but I found that people weren't making the connection between Debbie Kesling and Granny's Locket. When I decided to make miniature bears exclusively, I chose to change my business name. With the business name "Bears by Debbie Kesling," there is no doubt who the artist is! Select your business name carefully. It should reflect what you wish to convey. Read the teddy bear magazines and books that are on the market to help you avoid settling on a name that is already in use.

The rules governing businesses vary from state to state. Do all you can to insure that you are playing by the rules. You may need to register your business name. You will more than likely need a resale license. Some local governments have special requirements, as well. Contact the Small Business Administration for assistance.

Business Cards

Just as an art enthusiast can tell a Rubens from a Raphael, the seasoned "arctophile" can tell a Kilby from a Kesling. As you have probably discovered by now, your bears have a particular look that sets them apart from all others. Make this individuality a common thread that ties your business together.

Business cards are essential. They can be as simple or as elaborate as you wish. Consider adding a caricature or line art drawing of your bears to the card. The most productive card I ever used was a photo business card that featured a closeup of one of my bear's faces. Photo cards are expensive, but worth it.

Hang Tags

You should mark your bears in some way to show you designed them. On full-size bears, it's common for an artist to sign the footpads of the bears he or she makes. This can be difficult on very tiny bears. Design a tag of some sort to attach to your bears. Paper tags are fine, and some artists use shrink plastic to create unique tags for their work. Whatever type tag you use, try to keep it small so it doesn't overwhelm or detract from your bear. If you intend to use shrink plastic for your hang tags, be sure you use a ⅛" hole punch to make the thread hole before baking.

This 1¼" (about 3cm) bear is surrounded by the hang tags I used on my bears from the early to mid-1990s. Crafted from a special plastic that shrinks when baked, these tags are fun and easy to make.

Pricing

Now that your bears are ready for the marketplace, you must be ready for the inevitable question: "How much is that *darling* bear?" Prices on the market vary greatly. It seems to depend upon what the artist needs most from his or her sales. For some, selling a great number of bears is more important than making a lot of money. For others, teddy bears are how they make their living. Artists realize they must make a certain amount of money for each hour of their time.

There are three price ranges in the miniature bear market: low (up to $90), medium ($90-$150) and high (more than $150). How your bears fit into these ranges is something only you can decide. My lowest priced bears as of this printing are $150. The reasons for this are time, supply and demand. It takes me about eight and a half hours to complete a simple 2″ (5cm) bear. To justify giving up my real job to make bears for a living, I knew I needed to gross $20 an hour. This would allow me to clear about $13 an hour. Multiply the number of hours of labor spent on the bear by the $20 per hour rate and you get $170. If a bear is particularly elaborate and takes more time, adjusting the price is easy, provided you keep track of the time invested. The supply of my bears is very limited, and the demand is, thankfully, very high. If I awoke one day to find I had piles of bears sitting around with no one to adopt them, I would need to take a critical look at my bears (to see if my quality was slipping) and my prices (in comparison to the prices of other bears of similar quality).

If you price your bears too low, a surprising thing may happen: People may overlook your under-priced bears because they subconsciously think something must be wrong with them! Below-average prices also convey the feeling that you don't value your work, and if you don't value what you do, who will?

Price your bears too high, and the result is simple: They won't sell. Part of what allows an artist to ask higher than average prices for their work is reputation. You build reputation over time, not overnight. Unless your bears are simply extraordinary, don't expect to sell them for $200 or more right away.

It will take some experimenting, but you will know you have found the optimum price for your work if you cannot quite keep up with requests. Many artists will tell you that pricing their work is one of the most difficult aspects of the business.

Brochures

Once you have made the existence of your bears known to collectors through advertising, free publicity, shows or word of mouth, these collectors will often ask for a brochure or photos of what you have available. If you are doing open editions or large limited editions of particular designs, you should consider creating a pamphlet to offer to potential customers. If you have a home computer and printer, you can put together a nice brochure yourself. With the addition of a scanner and a color printer, you can do an even better job. If you don't have the time, desire or means to handle the task yourself, check the telephone book for printers who will do the job for you.

Whether you create a brochure on your own or have one created for you, be sure it contains all the information people need to make a decision and place an order. Color photographs are a plus, and complete descriptions of each bear are imperative. Provide as much information about each bear as you can. Here are some points you should cover in your descriptions:

- name of the bear
- size (from the bottom of the feet to the top of the head, not including ears)
- materials used (include both "fur" fabric and pawpads in the description)
- color (try to be as descriptive as possible)
- eyes (Are the eyes beads? Glass eyes on wires?)
- jointing (Is the bear string jointed or wire and disk jointed?)
- special features (Is this a no-no bear? Does it contain a secret compartment? Does the bear have a four-piece body or center-seam head? Can it be worn as a pin? Does it come with a certificate? Is it signed?)
- edition (Is this a limited edition? If so, how many are being made and which number of the edition is this particular bear? Is it an open edition? A one-of-a-kind?)
- price

It's nice to have an information packet ready so you can quickly respond to requests for information. One of my packets included a form letter, business card and two multiple-image photos of my work.

In addition to the descriptions of your bears, you should also let the readers know what your payment policies are. Do you require a deposit? If so, how much? When is the balance due? What forms of payment do you accept? Checks? Money orders? Credit cards? Do you require payment in your own national currency? Do you offer a layaway plan? If so, how does it work?

You also need to give customers all the information they need to pay you the correct amount. How do you handle the shipping charge? Is it based upon the dollar amount of the sale, the number of bears that are being purchased or weight? Do you offer shipping options, such as Priority Mail,

UPS, FedEx? If you offer shipping by UPS, remember that they will not deliver to a post office box and note that in your brochure. Is insurance included in the shipping charges? What shipping options do you offer for overseas customers?

What is your return policy? Are deposits nonrefundable? How long after a customer receives an order can she or he request a return? Can buyers return bears for a refund, or do you have an exchange-only policy?

By offering several ways for customers to place orders, you increase your sales dramatically. List on your brochure detailed instructions for order placement by any means possible: mail, phone,

fax, e-mail or World Wide Website. Providing an order form in your brochure will make it easy for customers to let you know what they want and easy for you to fill orders accurately.

A brief biography can be included in the brochure, as well. If your work has been shown in books and magazines, or if you have received any awards, include that information. You might want to mention how long you have been making bears, or what you did before bearmaking. Telling a little about yourself helps convey a feeling of familiarity. A nice photo of yourself can be a friendly touch, too!

If you do mostly one-of-a-kind bears, you may find it counterproductive to offer a brochure. Even if you make it very clear that the items shown in your brochure are not available, and that they are simply meant to be representative of your style and workmanship, people will want to order them. Until your work becomes widely known, it is helpful to make photos available of each piece you offer for sale. An instant camera will do the job, although the quality of the photos won't be suitable for most other purposes.

Brochures and photos can be costly to produce, so many artists charge a fee for them. It is common practice to refund this fee with the customer's first order. Once a person establishes herself as a buyer, it is customary to place her on your complimentary mailing list so she receives updates or new brochures at no charge. A computer comes in handy for keeping track of your mailing lists, orders pending and orders filled.

PHOTOGRAPHY

Potential customers, magazine editors and others will need photographs of your bears. Taking great pictures of miniatures is not easy. Here are some points you should keep in mind to help you get the super shots you need to promote your work.

Keep the background simple. Although it is tempting to clutter up your pictures with props and fancy backgrounds, these things only detract from the focal point: your bear. One exception to this rule is using a coin or other common object as a size reference in the picture.

Select a background color that complements your bear: A purple bear on a lime green background may not appeal to a wide audience. I use paper for bulletin boards that can be found in art and teacher's supply stores. It comes in a variety of colors, is inexpensive and photographs beautifully.

Bears don't always cooperate when you want to photograph them. Although it may seem easier to take pictures of a bear that is seated, limited depth-of-field makes it a challenge to get the whole bear in focus.

Many of my bears are self-standing, which means they will stand on their own without the additional support of a stand or strategically placed accessories. Self-standing or not, I always provide extra stability to a bear I am photographing by using needles in the back of the legs. Properly placed, the needles aren't visible to the camera, but allow you to easily reposition the bear. It's very frustrating to frame the perfect shot in the viewfinder only to have the bear topple over as you release the shutter!

Don't limit yourself to prints. Many publications insist upon slides or transparencies. It is a good idea to keep a supply of images on hand in several formats. Though 35mm slides are usually well received, 4″×5″ transparencies provide better color reproduction. It is common for an editor to request pictures from you with very little lead time. If you keep a supply of photos and slides on hand for opportunities with short notice, you will be one step ahead of artists who don't.

When photographing your bears, keep the background simple. Adding a common item that most people are familiar with, such as a thimble or coin, will help the viewer put the size of your piece into perspective.

I use quilting needles to give the bears (or bunnies) added stability during photo shoots.

Of course, photographing your work yourself isn't necessary. Professional photographers are available to do the job for you. Keep in mind that you will probably need to train the photographer a bit, no matter how skilled he or she is. Capturing the right look on a bear's face is an art in itself. Add to that the fact that miniatures are very difficult to photograph properly, and you can see that even this isn't an easy proposition.

Getting the Word Out

Now that you know what your prices will be, it's time to let people know that your bears exist. Here are several avenues through which you may publicize your work.

ADVERTISING

Advertising is the first path to publicity that most people think of. Color advertising in the bear magazines is costly, but beneficial. Both of the teddy bear magazines based in the United States have launched special advertising programs, designed for artists, which offer color ad space at a substantial savings. The only down side to these programs is that the ads are preformatted, meaning you supply a photo and text that the magazine inserts into an ad template. I feel the creative sacrifice is worth the benefit. Another pleasant benefit to these ads is that you needn't worry about getting color separations: The magazines do all the work for you. If you opt for a custom display ad, you will need to supply color separa-

rations for the publication's art department. Fortunately, the magazines offer these services at very reasonable prices.

What about black and white advertising? Though it is less expensive, black and white simply doesn't have the necessary impact to compete side-by-side with color. If you simply must run a black and white ad, consider purchasing the largest space you can afford.

Classified ads are, I feel, of limited benefit to the beginning artist. People need to see your work so that they can become familiar with it.

Don't overlook smaller publications when it comes to advertising. *Bear Tracks*, the official publication of Good Bears of the World, is a black and white production that goes out to thousands of people all over the world. Their advertising rates are very reasonable.

Many artists are forming co-ops to help lessen the financial burden of advertising. Several artists join forces and pay for a large color ad in one or more publications. Each participating artist's work is included in the ad, along with the appropriate contact information. This seems to be a workable arrangement, as more and more artists are advertising in this manner.

FREE PUBLICITY

There are many ways to get free publicity for your work. On a local level, offer to give teddy bear talks at libraries and schools. Teach some classes. Call the area newspapers, both large and small, and tell them about your bears. I did this once, and the resulting story was picked up by the Associated Press. Always carry one or more of your bears with you: You never know when an opportunity will present itself.

The teddy bear magazines are

By contacting local newspapers and sending photos through proper channels to the teddy bear magazines, you can gain a lot of free or nearly free publicity for your work.

another place where you can probably find some free promotion. *Teddy Bear and Friends* has a column written by Tracy Main that is devoted to miniatures. You send in photos and descriptions of your bears, and they may use them in the column. The same magazine has run a special feature the past few years called "Tribute to Tiny Teddies." They invite miniature bear artists to submit photos of their work for inclusion in this feature. *Teddy Bear Review* also invites artists to send pictures of their work for possible publication.

When dealing with the magazines, be professional, and try to avoid being pushy. The editors of these publications know their business. They don't need you to tell them how wonderful your bears are and why they should feature them in a six-page spread. If your bears are appealing, the appropriate individuals will spot your talent and will be eager to feature your work. Adorable bears (hopefully yours) sell magazines.

If your bears hit the right chord with the editors, and if you are extraordinarily lucky, they may ask that you provide a bear for a cover shot, which typically includes an accompanying article on you and your work. The magazines may also approach you for a feature article. If either of these things should happen, be prepared to handle many inquiries about your bears! When *Teddy Bear Review* featured my Grizzelda on the cover of their Spring 1991 issue, I received more than one hundred phone calls and upwards of five hundred letters.

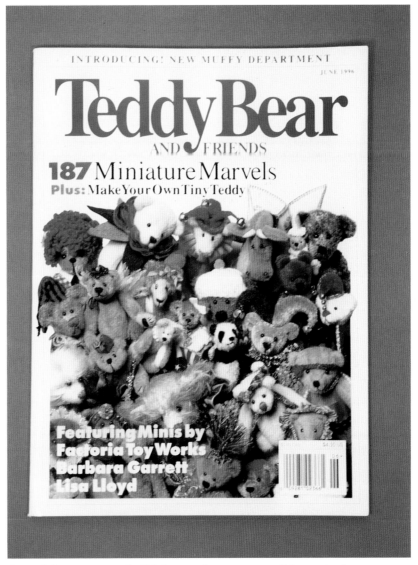

One of the most wonderful things about very small bears is that you can fit so many on a magazine cover! This is the Teddy Bear and Friends "Tribute to Tiny Teddies" issue for 1996.

NEARLY FREE PUBLICITY

Many bear clubs and shows host auctions to benefit various causes. One of the biggest in recent history was the auction to aid the victims of the Kobe/Osaka earthquake. Linda Mullins, well-known teddy bear collector and scholar, headed this effort. By donating a bear to such a cause, you get the benefit of exposure plus the "warm fuzzies" that come with helping those in need.

Another potential attention-getter is to enter contests sponsored by the teddy bear magazines. *Teddy Bear and Friends* magazine delivers the TOBY awards, and *Teddy Bear Review* handles the Golden Teddy Awards. I use the word "potential" because only the work of the finalists is featured in the publications. A nomination or win in either of these contests can play a big part in launching your career.

Being nominated for or winning a Golden Teddy or TOBY Award is a great boost for an artist's career and confidence. A panel of judges narrows the field of entries and readers select the winners.

NETWORKING

Linking with others in the teddy bear business world is accomplished in much the same way as in the "real" business world. The big difference is the teddy bear business world is a lot more fun. By networking, you will find new sources for supplies and new techniques to make your bears better, and you will make great friends with common interests. Whatever groups you belong to, try to remember it is a symbiotic relationship: Give at least as much as you get.

CLUBS

Although belonging to any bear club is both fun and beneficial, groups dedicated to miniature bears are of particular interest. The Tiny Teddy Lovers Club (TTLC) is a great group that offers a terrific newsletter, delightful tea parties, incredible learning experiences and unbeatable inspiration. They have a specific enrollment period, which means you may only join during a particular time of year.

Good Bears of the World (GBW) is the foremost bear-related benevolent organization in the world. Although the group focus isn't on miniature bears, you will meet the nicest teddy bear lovers in the world. My introduction to the world of bears was through Terrie Stong, now International Chairbear of this wonderful group.

SHOWS

I don't participate in many bear shows because it requires accumulating a stockpile of bears to offer for sale. This is something I am rarely able to do. I much prefer attending the shows as a visitor. This allows me to have fun looking around and talking with other artists. I have participated in some of the most valuable networking ever at 3:00 A.M. in a hotel room filled with artists, each of us sewing, or trimming a tiny face or adding just the right ribbon to a little bear. An artist once said, "You can't measure the success of a show in dollars and cents alone." How true!

When you participate in the larger shows, you have a good opportunity to be "discovered." Representatives from the prominent collector publications attend, as do scouts from manufacturers. Foreign collectors may purchase one of your pieces and pick up a bundle of your business cards to

The Tiny Teddy Lovers Club (T.T.L.C.) and Good Bears of the World (GBW) offer publications to members, and are good organizations to join. TTLC is devoted to miniature bears, and GBW is populated with warm, sharing members.

Shows, shows everywhere! But how to choose? Talk with other artists and ask what their experiences have been. Most artists will tell you honestly if a show was well attended, even if they personally didn't have good sales.

give to friends when they return home. Retailers are always on the lookout for new talent at these exhibitions, so have your wholesale game plan laid out before you get there, if you intend to seek out accounts with retailers.

Wholesale vs. Retail

Each of your bear sales will probably fall into one of two categories: retail or wholesale. Retail sales are those sales that you make directly to the public, either through your ads, at shows or via direct mailings. When you sell to a store or through a representative, you will probably sell wholesale. Both types of sales have pros and cons. You will need to decide for yourself what balance between the two will work best for you.

WHOLESALE

When you think wholesale, do you automatically figure you will need to sell your work for 50 percent of its retail price? Well, that's not necessarily true. They call the 50 percent mark in the wholesale/retail game *keystoning*. Ideally, a retailer wants to be able to double the price of what they buy. If your bear sells for $120 retail, the shop owner hopes to buy it from you for $60. This way of thinking works great for mass-produced items, but I feel that for unique, labor-intensive artwork such as bears, a different plan is in order, especially for established artists. Always try to negotiate.

For a beginning artist, connecting with a store owner who is particularly fond of the artist's work may be beneficial. Perhaps the owner will run advertising featuring the artist's bears. Maybe an in-store signing can be arranged. If the store participates in shows, will the owner take the artist's work along? All these things give added value to the relationship for the artist. If a shopkeeper agrees to truly promote your work, allow for that when you offer a percentage split.

If you arrange with a shop to sell to them at a discount less than 50 percent, don't be surprised if the owner still decides to sell your bears for double the price they paid. For example, if you sold the aforementioned $120 bear to a shop at a 70/30 split (in your favor), you would be paid $84. That gives the shop a $36 discount from your retail price. If the shop owner chooses to double the price they paid, your $120 bear has suddenly become a $168 bear that may sit and gather dust on the store shelf. Don't hesitate to ask what the store's policy is regarding pricing.

A fledgling artist should expect to wholesale at around the 50 percent mark, but remember: It is not carved in stone. If you don't feel comfortable negotiating with the shop owner, then perhaps it wouldn't be a good business arrangement in the long run. You need to have a good rapport with the people you do business with.

If you sell wholesale to shops, you need to provide those retailers with additional information. A simple way to handle this is to send your brochure to potential wholesale customers along with a reseller's information sheet which addresses some standard questions. Do you "keystone," that is, do you sell to retailers at 50 percent off the list price? Perhaps you offer resellers a flat percentage off list prices, such as 30 percent. (Another option is to have a sliding scale: the more a reseller purchases, the higher the percentage of discount.) Do you have a minimum order? Do you require the

retailer to promote your work in their magazine advertising in order for them to receive a particular discount? Are you willing and able to appear at the shop for showings or signings? Is a store-specific limited edition a possibility?

An attractive thing about selling through shops is that boxing up ten bears to send to one address is easier than having to send each of the ten bears to a different retail customer. Unfortunately, you will miss out on valuable feedback from the end buyer.

If your work is well received by the public, it's not uncommon for retailers to press for more output from you than you are comfortable with. Learning to say no is a difficult aspect of the business, one I still haven't mastered. I repeatedly over-extend myself, simply because I want to make everyone happy. Take my advice: Learn to set limits early on and stick with them! If you deal only with those retailers who make you feel comfortable, your life will be much simpler.

RETAIL SALES
By selling directly to the customer, you receive the full retail price for your work. You also get valuable feedback from the people who buy your bears. The nicest benefits are the friendships that develop. If you sell directly to the customer, however, you will find much of your bearmaking time gets used up on the phone and answering mail queries.

Mail Order
By running advertisements or sending out direct mail brochures

you are inviting people to contact you directly to purchase your bears. Keeping up with the requests for information can be tedious and time consuming. If you make mostly one-of-a-kind pieces as I do, a brochure is counterproductive.

Selling at Shows
Participating in shows is exciting, fun, hard work and, hopefully, profitable! Your profit margin is less than with mail order. You pay to enter, you pay to get yourself and your bears there, you pay for hotel and meals, and you lose valuable work time. But the up side is that shows offer you the opportunity to literally put your bears in the hands of the consumer. Prices for table space at shows vary, but most often it is well worth the price. Promoters typically schedule their shows to fall on or close to the same weekend each cycle. Some of these shows are legendary: the spring ABC show in Schaumburg, Illinois; the fall show in Timonium, Maryland (put on by D.L. Harrison and Co.); the Linda Mullins shows in San Diego, California. Waiting lists are not uncommon for these and other well-promoted teddy bear events. Sales can be brisk at these shows, so expect to have upwards of thirty bears ready to take with you.

Selling on the Internet
The latest venue for showcasing your work is the Information Superhighway, or Internet. E-mail mailing lists devoted to teddy bears and automatic links to teddy bear shops, artists and collectors worldwide make the Internet a

very promising marketplace. As part of your membership, many service providers include space to set up a homepage. This is your own little corner of cyberspace that you can customize to fit your needs and personality. My homepage has a display of my bears, of course, but it also includes hyperlinks to most of the other teddy bear sites online. I have also established an online gallery to showcase the work of bear artists who don't have a homepage. My "Cybearstore" is a popular place to shop for the latest teddy bear books and miniature bear making supplies.

The immediacy of e-mail makes it a wonderful way to do business. I have become so spoiled by the ease of online selling that the majority of the bears I make now find new homes this way. Overseas orders that used to require multiple phone calls, faxes and letters can be handled in the blink of an eye. (You can learn more about the teddy bear side of the Internet by reading my "Cybearspace" column in *Teddy Bear and Friends* magazine.)

The World Wide Web on the Internet provides a fantastic venue for showcasing your work.

Bear Gallery

"Pom Pom" is a 3" (7½cm) mohair bear by Alicia Albino of Australia.

This little 2½" (6cm) gold teddy was designed and created by artist Catherine Arlin.

"T.R." is a teddy bear representation of Theodore Roosevelt by Celia Baham. He stands 2½" (6cm) tall.

"BJ and his bear," by Edie Barlishen, is 3" (7½cm) tall. His little friend is just 1¼" (3cm).

Celia Baham's 2½" (6cm) "Maggie" wears a tiny hat and dress that Celia crocheted.

"Itsy" and "Bitsy," Sweetheart Bears by Edie Barlishen, are 1⅞" (about 47mm) and 1¾" (about 44mm), respectively. Note the charming, hand-stitched outfits.

3" (7cm) "Ben" by Anne Booth is a limited edition of four.

*"Little Bear" by Barb Butcher stands barely 1⅞"
(47mm) tall.*

*This charming little bear, "Duckie," has a very teddy
bear-ish look about him. He was created by artist Cathy
Cheung.*

"Bea Anne Angel" is a 2¾" (6½cm) bit of heaven crafted by Sandy Coombs. Sandy also created the harp and halo.

Margaret Crossland's little bear is about 2" (5cm) tall, and is holding a tiny Raggedy Ann doll that Margaret crocheted. Margaret creates incredible tiny "sock monkeys," Golliwogs and dolls, too!

*Use your imagination when selecting fabrics!
"Peppermint" by Janet Desjardine is 2¾" (6½cm) tall,
and features pawpads of floral print cotton.*

*"Josh", a 3" (7cm) miniature by Jutta Cyr, "bears" a
striking resemblance to Jutta's full-size bears.*

Terri Effan's "Pumpkin" shows creative use of the roly-poly idea. Terri has designed many roly-polys, including a line featuring seasonal themes. From the collection of Sandy Humanski.

"Li'l Bit" is a cute 2¼" (5½cm) teddy by Janet Desjardine.

Lorraine Garner's 2¼" (5½cm) "Fairy Bear" has wings and embellishments created from antique trim that has been hand-painted.

"Sleepy Bear" by Lorraine Garner is ready for bed in his perfectly scaled pajamas. He is 2¼" (5½cm) tall.

Loris Hancock's 3" (7½cm) "Sun Dappled Leaf Litter Bear" is from her "Rainforest Series" of work. This bear is a one-of-a-kind piece.

"Ashley" is a one-of-a-kind 2" (5cm) bear from the studio of Loris Hancock. Charming!

This 2½" (6cm) little girl was created by Denise Ilmanen, a California artist.

Mena Johnson has used a synthetic suede insert to give "Jester" a unique look. This piece is 3" (7½cm) tall, including his hat. He carries a marotte that was made utilizing the same insert technique.

"Molly" is 2¼" (5½cm), and has painted patchwork pawpads with decorative stitching. She was created by Kelli Kilby.

"Cream Ted," by Rita Loeb, is 2½" (6cm) and is stuffed with shot.

"Neville," by Randy Martin, is a dainty 2" (5cm) bear with an inset synthetic suede muzzle.

"Denver" is a 2¼" (5½cm) bear crafted by Randy Martin from fabric that he hand-dyed. Randy loves to experiment with dye, and many of his pieces are one-of-a-kind colors!

"Princess Jabeara" is a delightful 2½" (6cm) bear by artist Diane Pease. She created a limited edition of ten.

This 2½" (6cm) teddy named "Heather" is the first of an edition of ten. "Heather" was created by Louise Peers. From the author's collection.

Artist, author and photographer Carol-Lynn Rössel Waugh created this darling 3" (7½cm) mohair pair: "Mascot" and "Maria". Carol-Lynn is an artist who is able to successfully translate her full-size designs to miniature scale.

This 3" (7½cm) bear by Lesley Stipanov is named "Toggle." Note the decorative stitching around the footpads—a delightful touch!

"Baby Bear" by Lesley Stipanov is aptly named. Wide-set eyes and shortened limbs do give a bear a "baby" look. He is 2½" (6cm) tall.

This 2½" (6cm) little fellow, "Snowflake," was created by Trudy Yelland. In addition to her bears, Trudy makes wonderful Golliwogs.

When contacting artists, it is courteous to include a SASE (self-addressed stamped envelope) for their reply. When contacting artists overseas, ask your post office about International Reply Coupons.

If a telephone or fax number is listed, feel free to contact the artists in this way, but remember to take into consideration the time zones they live in. E-mail addresses are also listed for some of the artists, but "bear" in mind that the Internet is a dynamic environment, and things such as e-mail addresses can change frequently.

Please remember that the artist designs in this book are protected by copyright law, so please don't duplicate the work you see here. Use the imagination shown by these artists as a springboard for your own creations.

Because artists may readjust their price range periodically, no prices are given for any of the items shown. All of these artists will be happy to send you information on their work.

Alicia Albino
Bear Shanks Bears
Unit 19-176
Tapleys Hill Rd.
Royal Park 5014
S. Australia
p. 100 "Pom Pom" © Alicia Albino

Catherine Arlin
threads and . . .
947 Fletcher Ln. #212
Hayward, CA 94544
USA
Phone: (510) 582-5531
p. 101 gold teddy © Catherine Arlin

Celia Baham
Celia's Teddies
1562 San Joaquin Ave.
San Jose, CA 95118
USA
Phone: (408) 266-8129
Fax: (408) 978-2888
p. 101 "TR" © Celia Baham
p. 102 "Maggie" © Celia Baham

Edie Barlishen
Bears by Edie
42 Greer Crescent
St. Albert, Alberta
Canada T8N 1T8
Phone: (403) 459-5786
p. 102 "BJ and his bear" © Eddie Barlishen
p. 103 "Itsy" and "Bitsy" © Eddie Barlishen

Anne Booth
Chadwick Bears
22 Koromiko Rd..
Wanganui, New Zealand
Phone/Fax: 64-63-450-616
p. 103 "Ben" © Anne Booth

Barbara Butcher
Heartspun Teddy Bears
6801 - 59 Ave. Apt. #502
Red Deer, Alberta
Canada T4P 1B3
Phone: (403) 342-6686
p. 104 "Little Bear" © Barbara Butcher

Cathy Cheung
Larious Bears
#112-7633 St. Albans Rd.
Richmond, B.C.
Canada V6Y 3W7
Phone: (604) 244-0886
Fax: (604) 244-8647
E-mail: 102152.173@compuserve.com
p. 104 "Duckie" © Cathy Cheung

Sandy Coombs
Sandy's Bears
'Ailsa'
R.D. 54.
Kimbolton, New Zealand
Phone/Fax: 64-63-229-839
p. 105 "Bea Anne Angel" © Sandy Coombs

Margaret Crossland
30 Aptos Ave.
San Francisco, CA 94127
USA
Phone: (415) 584-9394
p. 105 little bear © Margaret Crossland

Jutta Cyr
Bearaphanalia Bears
343 Manora Rd. NE
Calgary, Alberta
Canada T2A 4R7
Phone: (403) 248-9231
Fax: (403) 248-9399
E-mail: cyrhuot@nucleus.com
p. 106 "Josh" © Jutta Cyr

Janet Desjardine
Tiny Teddies
580 Thirteenth St. N.W., Ste. 206
Portage La Prairie, Manitoba
Canada R1N 3R2
Phone: (204) 857-9202
p. 106 "Peppermint" © Janet Desjardine
p. 107 "Li'l Bit" © Janet Desjardine

Terri Effan
Terri's Baskets and Bears
1280 S. Raisinville Rd.
Monroe, MI 48161
USA
Phone: (313) 242-5601
E-mail: teffan@tdi.net
p. 107 "Pumpkin" © Terri Effan

Lorraine Garner
Lorraine's Hand Stitched Teddys
3590 Sacramento St., Apt. 2
San Francisco, CA 94118
USA
Phone: (415) 931-3674
p. 108 "Fairy Bear" © Lorraine
Garner
p. 99 and p. 108 "Sleepy Bear"
Lorraine Garner

Loris Hancock
Studio Seventy
"The Pines" Shopping Centre
Suite 370, Shop 80
Elanora QLD 4223
Australia
Phone: 07-5598-2242
Fax: 07-5525-6354
E-mail: minibear@OntheNet
.com.au
p. 109 "Sun Dappled Leaf Litter
Bear" © Loris Hancock
p. 109 "Ashley" © Loris Hancock

Denise Ilmanen
Galloping Bears
907 Sunnybrae Ln.
Novato, CA 94947
USA
Phone: (415) 898-1427
Fax: (415) 461-3386
E-mail: Dilmanen@midas.org
p. 110 little girl © Denise Ilmanen

Mena Johnson
Meke Bears
P.O. Box 274
Mosman
N.S.W.
Australia 2088
Phone: 02-9969-4430
Fax: 02-9969-5555
p. 110 "Jester" © Mena Johnson

Debbie Kesling
Bears by Debbie Kesling
8429 Lambert Dr.
Lambertville, MI 48144-9785
USA
Phone: (313) 856-HUGS(4847)
Fax: (313) 856-7197
E-mail: debbie@cybearspace
.com
Homepage: http://www
.cybearspace.com/

Kelli Kilby
Kelli's Kollectibles
P.O. Box 2824
Rancho Cucamonga, CA 91729
USA
Phone: (909) 980-3887
Fax: (909) 941-4607
p. 111 "Molly" © Kelli Kilby

Rita Loeb
Rita Loeb's Tiny Teddy Company
2995 Van Buren Blvd.
A13-145
Riverside, CA 92503
USA
Phone: (909) 780-9410
Fax: (909) 780-5141
E-mail: Tbirdtom@aol.com
p. 111 "Cream Ted" © Rita Loeb

Randy Martin, Sr.
Lil' Brother's Bears
3212 135th St.
Toledo, OH 43611
USA
Phone: (419) 729-0206
p. 112 "Neville" © Randy Martin
p. 112 "Denver" © Randy Martin

Diane Pease
Piece by Pease Teddy Bears
328 Huffman Dr.

Exton, PA 19341
USA
Phone/Fax: (610) 363-9391
E-mail: dcpbears@onit.net
p. 113 "Princess Jabeara" © Diane
Pease

Louise Peers
71 Gravel Ln.
Wilmslow
Cheshire SK96LS
England
Phone: 01625 532320
p. 113 "Heather" © Louise Peers

Carol-Lynn Rössel Waugh
5 Morrill St.
Winthrop, ME 04364-1220
USA
Phone: (207) 377-6769
Fax: (207) 377-4158
p. 114 "Mascot" and "Maria" ©
Carol-Lynn Rössel Waugh

Lesley Stipanov
Les Bears
92 Terowi St.
Sunnybank Hills
Queensland
Australia 4109
Phone: 07-3345-9316
p. 114 "Toggle" © Lesley Stipanov
p. 115 "Baby Bear" © Lesley
Stipanov

Trudy Yelland
Tru's Bearables
132 Tisdale St. N.
Hamilton, Ontario
Canada L8L 5M6
Phone: (905) 528-0702
E-mail: trusbears@sympatico.ca
p. 115 "Snowflake" © Trudy
Yelland

*T*he projects in this book are intended to be starting points for you. Rather than thinking of the conclusion of this book as an ending, think of it as a beginning. Sit down with some graph paper and let your imagination run wild! And don't limit yourself to designing teddy bears: Many artists are creating incredible menageries that include everything from aardvarks to zebras.

You can see from the wonderful sampling of bears in section four that there are as many styles as there are artists. Allow these works to inspire you. Your own personality will come through in the designs you create. It is very satisfying to know that you have created something so unique, so personal, it is recognized as your work at first glance. This satisfaction is just one of the many rewards that awaits you in the special world of miniature collectible bears.

Good luck to you, and above all, *have fun!*

Appendix A: Photographing Miniatures

by John Kesling

Photographing bears that are 3″ (7cm) tall and shorter is more complicated than you might think! Here are some guidelines to help you show off your hard work with the best results.

Don't expect good results with one of those compact point-and-shoot type cameras. They were designed for ease of use and don't work well for photographing miniatures. For best results you will need a single lens reflex camera (SLR) with through-the-lens metering. Autofocus and all the other "bells and whistles" are not required.

Use ASA 400 film. It provides a good balance between graininess and the speed required to get enough depth of field. I sometimes use ASA 200 or 100 if I know the photos will be greatly enlarged, which is often the case with photographs of miniatures.

Use a medium telephoto lens, 100mm to 150mm. Use a macro lens or you will need extension tubes or a bellows to enable you to focus closely enough. A fixed focal length macro lens is preferred over a zoom macro lens because most zoom macro lenses must be zoomed all the way out before you can use macro focus.

Use the smallest lens opening (highest F number) possible to achieve proper exposure. The smaller the lens opening, the greater the "depth of field." This just means that with smaller lens openings more of your shot will be in focus. This also means that you will be using long shutter times: one half second, one second, and even longer. For these longer exposures, you will need a tripod and a cable release.

If your camera has autofocus, you should disable it if possible. When adjusting focus, make certain your lens is open all the way (smallest F number). Most SLR cameras will do this automatically. With your lens open, more light will be allowed through to the viewfinder, giving you a brighter image. This also reduces the depth of field, so as you're focusing, be aware that more of the shot will be in focus on the film than you are seeing through the viewfinder. Slowly adjust the focus through the shot. As you do this, observe how different parts of the miniature come into focus. Try to set the focus halfway between the points where the closest and farthest parts came into focus. To check the focus, set the F stop to what you will be using to take the picture. The image in the viewfinder will get much darker, but as it does you will see more of the shot come into focus. You may have to "fudge" the focus in one direction or another to make sure the critical parts are in focus.

Don't mix light sources. Use either all natural light or all incandescent photo floods. Different types of light have different color temperatures and will change the colors in the photos. When you mix different types of light, it is impossible to determine how they will affect the colors in the finished product. Avoid using fluorescent lights: They vary too widely in color temperature.

If you use incandescent photo floods, be sure to use the appropriate filter on your lens to compensate for the color balance of the light. Your local camera shop can help you choose the right filter.

If you're using print film, take samples of your background material, and possibly even the miniature itself, when you have prints made. In almost all cases, the automatic machines used to print the pictures will be totally confused by the color balance and do a terrible job of selecting filters. If you provide samples, the operator can override the automatic settings and do a pretty good job of getting the colors right.

Metering systems in some cameras may be confused by strong light entering the viewfinder. Use care when positioning lights, or shield the viewfinder opening when the metering system is active.

Make certain the subject of your photo is "looking at you." Try to pose the bear so that it is looking into the camera. Positioning the bear so that a bit of light reflects off the eyes adds a bit of life to the shot.

As much fun as it can be tracking down elusive fabric and supplies, it is comforting to know that suppliers exist to do this leg work for us. Here are a few of the best sources I have found. I strongly urge you to purchase *The Teddy Bear Source Book*, as it contains the most complete listing of teddy bear suppliers ever compiled.

YLI Corporation
silk ribbon, beautiful threads
45 W. 300 North
Provo, UT 84601
Phone: (800) 854-1932

Tydd's Teddies
kits, patterns, fabrics and more
50 W. Fourth St.
Hamilton, Ontario
Canada L9C 3M4
Phone: (905) 385-6992
E-mail: tydd@netaccess.on.ca

The Abearondack Bear Company
Charles P. McGinnis
recycled glass pellets for stuffing bears
P.O. Box 308
Crosby Rd.
Madrid, NY 13660
Phone: (315) 322-4063
E-mail: teddyb@northweb.com
Home page: http://www
.north web.com/~teddyb/

Edinburgh Imports, Inc.
patterns, kits, fabrics and more
P.O. Box 722
Woodland Hills, CA 91365
Phone: (800) 334-6274 (U.S. and Canada)
Phone: (818) 591-3800 (within California)
E-mail: orders@edinburgh.com
Homepage: http://www
.edinburgh.com/

Emily Farmer
wonderful kits
P.O. Box 2911
Sanford, NC 27330
Fax: (919) 775-5365

Teddys by Tracy
nice selection of fabrics, eyes and more
32 Pikehall Pl.
Baltimore, MD 21236
Phone/Fax: (410) 529-2418

Field's Fabrics by Mail
fantastic source for synthetic suede
1695 Forty-fourth St. S.E.
Grand Rapids, MI 49508-5001
Phone: (616) 455-4570
Phone: (800) 67ULTRA

Lucky Squirrel Press
professional quality shrink plastic
1635 Menaul N.W.
Albuquerque, NM 87107
Phone: (800) 462-4912 (orders only)
E-mail: squirrel@Rt66.com

Many "arctophiles" (bear lovers) live in rural or remote areas, making it difficult to find others with whom to share their hobby. Even if you are fortunate enough to have a local bear club, the following organizations are fun and worthwhile. Much of the fun of making and collecting bears comes from the friendships that are formed through the hobby.

Good Bears of the World
P.O. Box 13097
Toledo, OH 43613-0097
Voice and Fax: (419) 531-5365

This benevolent organization provides teddy bears to those in need. Local "dens" exist in many areas, but there are also many members-at-large. Members receive a membership card, GBW button, and four issues (annually) of *Bear Tracks*, the newsletter of GBW.

Tiny Teddy Lovers Club
(T.T.L.C.)
℅ Terri Effan
1280 S. Raisinville Rd.
Monroe, MI 48161

Here are some wonderful books and magazines that will help you find supplies, locate other artists, research classic bear designs and track down just about everything you might want to learn about teddy bears in general. Though there are many other books available on teddies, these are the books I personally consider "must-haves."

The Teddy Bear Source Book
Edited by Argie Manolis
Published by Betterway Books,
1995
ISBN: 1-55870-386-1

Teddy Bear and Friends
Published six times a year by
Cowles Magazines
Subscription information:
(800) 829-3340 (U.S. and Canada)
(909) 446-6914 (other countries)

Teddy Bear Review
Published six times a year by
Collector Communications Corp.
Subscription information:
(800) 347-6969 (U.S. only)
(614) 382-3322 (other countries)

Collectors' Guide to Miniature Teddy Bears: Identification and Values
by Cynthia Powell
Published by Collector Books,
1993
ISBN: 0-89145-567-1

Teddy Bears Past and Present, Volume 2
by Linda Mullins
Published by Hobby House Press,
1992
ISBN: 0-87588-384-2

Contemporary Teddy Bear Price Guide: Artists to Manufacturers
by Terry and Doris Michaud
Published by Hobby House Press,
1992
ISBN: 0-87588-398-2

INDEX

A
Advertising, 94
Arms
   jointing, 39–40
   stuffing, for Roly-poly Bear, 51
Artists, miniature bear, 13–14, 116–117
Assembly
   Bunny, 86–88
   Roly-poly Bear, 52

B
Backstitch, 23
Basic Jointed Bear, 53–59
Basket tool, 20
Bear. *See* Miniature bear, Teddy bear
Body piece
   stuffing, for Roly-poly Bear, 51–52
   turning, right-side out, 25–27
   using backstitch to sew, 23
Brochures, 91–94
Bunny, 84–88
Business cards, 90
Business, naming, 90

C
Clubs, for teddy bear lovers, 122
   membership in, 96
Collar, bodice or ruffle, using running
   stitch with, 25
Construction
   miniature bear, 21–30
   Panda, 67
Construction, completing
   Jester Bear, 62
   No-no Bear, 82
   Santa Bear, 73
Cutting, 22
   Bunny, 85
   Posy Bear, 43
   Simple Teddy, 38
   Teddy Bear Pin, 35
   See also Scissors, Sidecutters

D
Damage, repairing, 31
Dykes. *See* Sidecutters

E
Ears
   attaching, 29–30
   Posy Bear, 46
   Simple Teddy, 39–41
   Teddy Bear Pin, 36
   using whipstitch to sew, 25
Effan, Terri, 20
Eye patches, for Panda, 68

Eyes, 18
   Basic Jointed Bear, 58
   mounting and seating, 27–28
   Simple Teddy, 39
   Teddy Bear Pin, 36
Eyes, placing, 28
   Posy Bear, 44–45

F
Fabric, 15–16
   dyeing, 43
   Panda, 66
Flower petals, for Posy Bear, 47–48

G
Gathering stitch, 25
Glue, 19
   applying, to damaged area, 32
Good Bears of the World, 96
Grooming, 31

H
Hang tags, 90
Head
   mounting, for Posy Bear, 45
   shaping, for Panda, 67
   Simple Teddy, 39
   stuffing, for Roly-poly Bear, 51
   turning, 35–36
Hemostats, 19–20
   for turning body piece right-side out,
   25–27
Hole punch, for disk joints, 17, 20

I
Ideal Toy Company, 12–13
Internet, selling on, 98–99

J
Jester Bear, 60–64
Jointing
   Basic Jointed Bear, 55–58
   head to body, 39–40
   Jester Bear, 62
   legs and arms, 39–40
   making disks for, 17
   No-no Bear, 81
   Santa Bear, 73
   string, 40

L
Ladder stitch, 24–25
Layout, 22
   Basic Jointed Bear, 54
   Bunny, 85
   Jester Bear, 61

No-no Bear, 79
Panda, 66–67
Posy Bear, 43
Roly-poly Bear, 50
Santa Bear, 71
Simple Teddy, 38
Teddy Bear Pin, 35
Legs, jointing, 39–40

M
Mail order, selling by, 98
Materials, 15–19
   Basic Jointed Bear, 54
   Bunny, 85
   importance of using high-quality, 15
   Jester Bear, 61
   No-no Bear, 79
   Panda, 66
   Posy Bear, 43
   for poupard, 63
   Roly-poly Bear, 50
   for Santa Bear's toy sack and bear, 76
   Simple Teddy, 38
   sources for, 121
   Teddy Bear Pin, 35
Mechanism, for No-no Bear, completing,
   82–83
Miniature bear
   construction of, 21–30
   defined, 14
   tiny, 76–77
Mouth
   and nose, 28
   Posy Bear, 46
   Teddy Bear Pin, 36

N
Neck, using running stitch with, 25
Needles, 19
Networking, 96
No-no Bear, 78–83
Nose
   creative colors for, 29
   and mouth, 28
   Posy Bear, 46
   Teddy Bear Pin, 36

P
Panda, 65–69
Pattern, 21–22
   Basic Jointed Bear, 54
   enlarging, 31
   Jester Bear, 61
   No-no Bear, 79
   Roly-poly Bear, 50

Santa Bear, 71
   stamping, 21–22
Pens and markers, 18–19
Photographs
   for marketing bears, 93–94
   tips for taking, 120
Pinback, attaching, for Teddy Bear Pin,
   36
Plastic bags, uses for, 18
Port, Beverly, 13
Port, Kimberlee, 14
Poster board, for tracing, 21
Posy Bear, 42–48
Poupard, making, for Jester Bear, 63–64
Pricing, 91
Publicity
   free, 94–95
   inexpensive, 95

R
Reflocking, 31–32
Repairs, using ladder stitch, 24
Retail. *See* Wholesale, vs. retail
Ribbon, 16–17
Roly-poly Bear, 49–52
Rubber stamps, for stamping patterns,
   21–22
Ruffles and flourishes, 62
Running stitch, 25

S
Santa Bear, 70–77
Schuco miniatures, 14
Scissors, 19
Seams, repairing ripped, 24
Sewing
   Basic Jointed Bear, 54–55
   Bunny, 86
   Jester Bear, 61
   No-no Bear, 79–80
   Posy Bear, 43–44
   Roly-poly Bear, 50
   Santa Bear, 72
   Simple Teddy, 38
   Teddy Bear Pin, 35
   See also Stitching
Shading, Posy Bear, 46
Shows
   exhibiting in, 96–97
   selling at, 98
Sidecutters, 19–20
Simple Teddy, 37–41
Steiff, Margaret, 13
Stitching, 22–25
String jointing, 40
Stuffing, 17–18, 27
   Basic Jointed Bear, 58
   closing after, 24
   Panda, 68
   Posy Bear, 44–45

   Roly-poly Bear, 51–52
   Simple Teddy, 38
   Teddy Bear Pin head, 35–36

T
Teddy bear
   artist-designed, 13
   brief history of, 12–14
Teddy Bear Pin, 34–36
Teddy Girl, 13
Thread, 16
   for stitching nose, 28
Tiny Teddy Lovers Club, 96
Tools, 19–20
Toy sack, for Santa Bear, 76–77
Tracing, 22
Trim, 16–17
   attaching, for Teddy Bear Pin, 36
   for Panda, 69
   for Roly-poly Bear, 52
   for Santa Bear, 74–75
Trimming, as final touch, 41
Tweezers, 19–20

W
Whipstitch, 25
   ears, 29–30
Wholesale, vs. retail, 97–99
Wires, for joints, 17

More Great Books for Creating Beautiful Crafts

Creating Extraordinary Beads From Ordinary Materials—Transform the most ordinary, accessible materials into uncommonly beautiful beads! You'll be amazed at the fascinating array of beads you can create using these 53 step-by-step projects in a range of styles—and no experience or fancy equipment is needed! #30905/$22.99/128 pages/326 color, 18 b&w illus./paperback

Painting Flowers in Watercolor With Louise Jackson—Master decorative artist, Louise Jackson, shows you how to beautifully render one of decorative painting's most popular subjects—flowers! All you need is the desire to follow 15 detailed, step-by-step projects from start to finish! #30913/$23.99/128 pages/165 color, 21 b&w illus./paperback

Creative Finishes Series—Explore the world of creative finishing with leading decorative artist, Phil Myer! Each book features a variety of techniques, paint applications and surface treatments in 15 projects complete with detailed instructions, patterns and step-by-step photos.
   Painting & Decorating Tables—#30910/ $23.99/112 pages/177 color illus./ paperback
   Painting & Decorating Boxes—#30911/ $23.99/112 pages/145 color, 32 b&w illus./paperback

Gretchen Cagle's Decorative Painting Keepsakes—Discover a treasury of beautiful projects collected from one of today's most celebrated decorative painters! In her latest book, Gretchen shares 31 of her all-time favorite projects. No matter what your skill level, clear instructions, traceable patterns and color mixing recipes will have you painting in no time! #30975/$24.99/144 pages/91 color, 44 b&w illus./paperback

The Crafter's Guide to Pricing Your Work—Price and sell more than 75 kinds of crafts with this must-have reference. You'll learn how to set prices to maximize income while maintaining a fair profit margin. Includes tips on record-keeping, consignment, taxes, reducing costs and managing your cash flow. #70353/$16.99/160 pages/paperback

Selling Your Dolls and Teddy Bears: A Complete Guide—Earn as you learn the business, public relations and legal aspects of doll and teddy bear sales. Some of the most successful artists in the business share the nitty-gritty details of pricing, photographing, tax planning, customer relations and more! #70352/$18.99/ 160 pages/31 b&w illus./paperback

The Teddy Bear Sourcebook: For Collectors and Artists—Discover the most complete treasury of bear information stuffed between covers. You'll turn here whenever you need to find sellers of bear making supplies, major manufacturers of teddy bears, teddy bear shows, auctions and contests, museums that house teddy bear collections and much more. #70294/ $18.99/356 pages/202 illus./paperback

Painting & Decorating Birdhouses—Turn unfinished birdhouses into something special—from a quaint Victorian roost to a Southwest pueblo, from a rustic log cabin to a lighthouse! These colorful and easy decorative painting projects are for the birds with 22 clever projects to create indoor decorative birdhouses, as well as functional ones to grace your garden. #30882/$23.99/128 pages/194 color illus./paperback

How to Start Making Money With Your Crafts—Launch a rewarding crafts business with this guide that starts with the basics—from creating marketable products to setting the right prices—and explores all the exciting possibilities. End-of-chapter quizzes, worksheets, ideas and lessons learned by successful crafters are included to increase your learning curve. #70302/$18.99/176 pages/35 b&w illus./paperback.

Painting Houses, Cottages and Towns on Rocks—Turn ordinary rocks into charming cottages, country churches and Victorian mansions! Accomplished artist Lin Wellford shares 11 fun, inexpensive, step-by-step projects that are sure to please. #30823/$21.99/ 128 pages/398 color illus./paperback

The Doll Sourcebook—Bring your dolls and supplies as close as the telephone with this unique sourcebook of retailers, artists, restorers, appraisers and more! Each listing contains extensive information—from addresses and phone numbers to business hours and product lines. #70325/$22.99/352 pages/176 b&w illus./paperback

Making Greeting Cards With Rubber Stamps—Discover hundreds of quick, creative, stamp-happy ways to make extra-special cards—no experience, fancy equipment or expensive materials required! You'll find 30 easy-to-follow projects for holidays, birthdays, thank you's and more! #30821/ $21.99/128 pages/231 color illus./paperback

How to Make Clay Characters—Bring cheery clay characters to life! The creator of collectible clay "Pippsywoggins" figures shares her fun and easy techniques for making adorable little figures—no sculpting experience required! #30881/$22.99/128 pages/579 color illus./paperback

The Art of Jewelry Design—Discover a colorful showcase of the world's best contemporary jewelers. This beautiful volume illustrates the skilled creative work of 21 production jewelers, featuring a wide variety of styles, materials and techniques. #30826/$29.99/144 pages/300 color illus.

Making Books by Hand—Discover 12 beautiful projects for making handmade albums, scrapbooks, journals and more. Only everyday items like cardboard, wrapping paper and ribbon are needed to make these exquisite books for family and friends. #30942/$24.99/108 pages/250 color illus.

Make It With Paper Series—Discover loads of bright ideas and easy-to-do projects for making colorful paper creations. Includes paper to cut and fold, templates and step-by-step instructions for designing your own creations. Plus, each paperback book has over 200 color illustrations to lead you along the way.
   Paper Boxes—#30935/$19.99/114 pages
   Paper Pop-Ups—#30936/$19.99/96 pages

Make Jewelry Series—With basic materials and a little creativity you can make great-looking jewelry! Each 96-page paperback book contains 15 imaginative projects using materials from clay to fabric to paper—and over 200 color illustrations to make jewelry creation a snap!
   Make Bracelets—#30939/$15.99
   Make Earrings—#30940/$15.99
   Make Necklaces—#30941/$15.99

Acrylic Decorative Painting Techniques—Discover stroke-by-stroke instruction that takes you through the basics and beyond! More than 50 fun and easy painting techniques are illustrated in simple demonstrations that offer at least two variations on each method. Plus, a thorough discussion on tools, materials, color, preparation and backgrounds. #30884/$24.99/128 pages/550 color illus.

The Decorative Stamping Sourcebook—Embellish walls, furniture, fabric and accessories—with stamped designs! You'll find 180 original, traceable motifs in a range of themes and illustrated instructions for making your own stamps to enhance any decorating style. #30898/$24.99/128 pages/200 color illus.

The Best of Silk Painting—Discover inspiration in sophisticated silk with this gallery of free-flowing creativity. Over 100 full-color photos capture the glorious colors, unusual textures and unique designs of 77 talented artists. #30840/$29.99/128 pages/136 color illus.

Master Strokes—Master the techniques of decorative painting with this comprehensive guide! Learn to use decorative paint finishes on everything from small objects and furniture to walls and floors, including dozens of step-by-step demonstrations and numerous techniques. #30937/$22.99/160 pages/400 color illus./paperback

Decorative Painting Sourcebook—Priscilla Hauser, Phillip Myer and Jackie Shaw lend their expertise to this one-of-a-kind guide straight from the pages of *Decorative Artist's Workbook*! You'll find step-by-step, illustrated instructions on every technique—from basic brushstrokes to faux finishes, painting glassware, wood, clothing and much more! #30883/$24.99/128 pages/200 color illus./ paperback

The Art of Painting Animals on Rocks—Discover how a dash of paint can turn humble stones into charming "pet rocks." This hands-on easy-to-follow book offers a menagerie of fun—and potentially profitable—stone animal projects. Eleven examples, complete with material lists, photos of the finished piece and patterns will help you create a forest of fawns, rabbits, foxes and other adorable critters. #30606/$21.99/144 pages/250 color illus./ paperback

Fabric Sculpture: The Step-by-Step Guide & Showcase—Discover how to transform fabrics into 3-dimensional images. Seven professional fabric sculptors demonstrate projects that illustrate their unique approaches and methods for creating images from fabric. The techniques—covered in easy, step-by-step illustration and instruction—include quilting, thread work, applique and soft sculpture. #30687/$29.99/160 pages/300+ color illus.

Decorative Wreaths & Garlands—Discover stylish, yet simple-to-make wreaths and garlands. These 20 original designs use fabrics and fresh and dried flowers to add color and personality to any room, and charm to special occasions. Clear instructions are accompanied by step-by-step photographs to ensure that you create a perfect display every time. #30696/ $19.99/96 pages/175 color illus./paperback

Paper Craft—Dozens of step-by-step paper craft projects to make, including greeting cards, boxes and desk sets, jewelry and pleated paper blinds. If you have ever worked with or wanted to work with paper you'll enjoy these attractive, fun-to-make projects. #30530/ $16.95/144 pages/200 color illus./paperback

Jewelry & Accessories: Beautiful Designs to Make and Wear—Discover how to make unique jewelry out of papier maché, wood, leather, cloth and metals. You'll learn how to create: a hand-painted wooden brooch, a silk-painted hair slide, a paper and copper necklace and much more! Fully-illustrated with step-by-step instructions. #30680/$17.99/128 pages/150 color illus./paperback

Elegant Ribboncraft—Over 40 ideas for exquisite ribbon-craft—hand-tied bows, floral garlands, ribbon embroidery and more. Various techniques are employed—including folding, pleating, plaiting, weaving, embroidery, patchwork, quilting, applique and decoupage. All projects are complete with step-by-step instructions and photographs. #30697/$16.99/ 128 pages/130+ color illus./paperback

Nature Craft—Dozens of step-by-step nature craft projects to create, including dried flower garlands, baskets, corn dollies, potpourri and more. Bring the outdoors inside with these wonderful projects crafted with readily available natural materials. #30531/$16.99/144 pages/200 color illus./paperback

Create Your Own Greeting Cards and Gift Wrap With Priscilla Hauser—You'll see sponge prints, eraser prints, cellophane scrunching, marbleizing, paper making and dozens of other techniques you can use to make unique greetings for all your loved ones. #30621/$24.99/128 pages/230 color illus.

Creative Paint Finishes for Furniture—Revive your furniture with fresh color and design! Inexpensive, easy and fun painting techniques are at your fingertips, along with step-by-step directions and a photo gallery of imaginative applications for faux finishing, staining, stenciling, mosaic, découpage and many other techniques. #30748/$27.99/144 pages/236 color, 7 b&w illus.

The Crafts Supply Sourcebook: A Comprehensive Shop-by-Mail Guide, 4th Edition—Turn here to find the materials you need—from specialty tools and the hardest-to-find accessories, to clays, doll parts, patterns, quilting machines and hundreds of other items! Listings organized by area of interest make it quick and easy! #70344/$18.99/320 pages/paperback

Master Works: How to Use Paint Finishes to Transform Your Surroundings—Discover how to use creative paint finishes to enhance and excite the "total look" of your home. This step-by-step guide contains dozens of exciting ideas on fresco, marbling, paneling and other simple paint techniques for bringing new life to any space. Plus, you'll also find innovative uses for fabrics, screens and blinds. #30626/$29.95/176 pages/150 color illus.

Everything You Ever Wanted to Know About Fabric Painting—Discover how to create beautiful fabrics! You'll learn how to set up workspace, choose materials, plus the ins and outs of tie-dye, screen printing, woodgraining, marbling, cyanotype and more! #30625/$21.99/128 pages/4-color throughout/paperback

Creative Paint Finishes for the Home—A complete, full-color, step-by-step guide to decorating floors, walls and furniture—including how to use the tools, master the techniques and develop ideas. #30426/$27.99/144 pages/212 color illus.

Creative Silk Painting—Uncover the secrets of silk painting as you get the inside story on how to apply brilliant color to silk and create beautiful art more quickly and easily. You'll explore exciting new topics, including new instant set dyes, creative painting techniques, creating garments and textile art and much more! #30713/$26.99/144 pages/120 color illus.

Stencil Source Book 2—Add color and excitement to fabrics, furniture, walls and more with over 200 original motifs that can be used again and again! Idea-packed chapters will help you create dramatic color schemes and themes to enhance your home in hundreds of ways. #30730/$22.99/144 pages/300 illus.

Paint Craft—Discover great ideas for enhancing your home, wardrobe and personal items. You'll see how to master the basics of mixing and planning colors, how to print with screen and linoleum to create your own stationery,

how to enhance old glassware and pottery pieces with unique patterns and motifs and much more! #30678/$16.95/144 pages/200 color illus./paperback

Decorative Painting With Gretchen Cagle—Discover decorative painting at its finest as you browse through pages of charming motifs. You'll brighten walls, give life to old furniture, create unique accent pieces and special gifts using step-by-step instructions, traceable drawings, detailed color mixes and more! #30803/$24.99/144 pages/64 color, 36 b&w illus./paperback

Painting Murals—Learn through eight step-by-step projects how to choose a subject for a mural, select colors that will create the desired effects and transfer the design to the final surface. #30081/$29.99/168 pages/125 color illus.

Decorative Boxes to Create, Give and Keep—Craft beautiful boxes using techniques including embroidery, stencilling, lacquering, gilding, shellwork, decoupage and many others. Step-by-step instructions and photographs detail every project. #30638/$15.95/128 pages/4-color throughout/paperback

Painting Baby Animals With Peggy Harris—Now you can paint adorable baby animals with the help of professional oil painter Peggy Harris! You'll learn her fun, exciting and virtually foolproof method of painting using 11 color, step-by-step projects that show you how to paint a variety of realistic little critters—from puppies and kittens to ducklings and fawns. #30824/$21.99/128 pages/ 319 color illus./paperback

Handmade Jewelry: Simple Steps to Creating Wearable Art—Create unique and wearable pieces of art—and have fun doing it! 42 step-by-step jewelry-making projects are at your fingertips—from necklaces and earrings, to pins and barrettes. Plus, no experience, no fancy equipment and no expensive materials are required! #30820/$21.99/128 pages/126 color, 30 b&w illus./paperback

Holiday Fun Year-Round With Dian Thomas—Discover how to turn mere holiday observances into opportunities to exercise imagination and turn the festivity all the way up. You'll find suggestions for a memorable New Year's celebration, silly April Fool's Day pranks, recipes and ideas for a Labor Day family get-together, creative Christmas giving and much more! #70300/$19.99/144 pages/150 color illus./paperback